Advance praise for
How to Love Someone Without Losing Your Mind

"A raw, real, and normalizing book about the inevitable challenges we face in relationships. Todd Baratz connects deeply with his reader by sharing his own story and those of his clients, offering a relatable perspective on the path toward loving another without losing your own individuality and sense of self."

—VIENNA PHARAON,
national bestselling author of *The Origins of You*
and host of the podcast *This Keeps Happening*

"Personal, honest, and provocative . . . Baratz challenges narratives, normalizes relationship challenges, and helps you build healthier dynamics. He is saying everything that needs to be said about love today."

—DR. SARA KUBURIC,
creator of MillennialTherapist
and author of *It's On Me*

"Love is 'unpredictable' and 'uncertain,' as Todd Baratz puts it in his candid and unequivocal new book. If you are looking for a road map to navigating the complexities of love today, this book is for you."

—ALEXANDRA H. SOLOMON, PhD,
faculty at Northwestern University,
bestselling author of *Love Every Day*,
and host of the podcast *Reimagining Love*

"Todd Baratz writes the truth about relationship dynamics that we all need to hear. Finally a therapist who tells it like it is and cuts through all the pop psychology dogma that's permeating the internet. This is a must-read for everyone."

—JILLIAN TURECKI

"Imagine receiving practical advice on how to change your life from your wise and hilarious best friend who happens to be a trained therapist. With wisdom, empathy, and humor, Todd Baratz will help you uplevel your relationships by first understanding the relationship with yourself."

—EMILY MORSE,
host of the podcast *Sex with Emily*,
doctor of human sexuality, and author of *Smart Sex*

HOW TO LOVE SOMEONE
WITHOUT LOSING YOUR MIND

HOW TO LOVE SOMEONE

WITHOUT LOSING YOUR MIND

Forget the Fairy Tale and Get Real

Todd Baratz, LMHC

RODALE
NEW YORK

Published in the United States by Rodale Books, an imprint of Random House, a division of Penguin Random House LLC, New York.

RODALE and the Plant colophon are registered trademarks of Penguin Random House LLC.

Library of Congress Cataloging-in-Publication Data
Names: Baratz, Todd, author.
Title: How to love someone without losing your mind: forget the fairy tale and get real / Todd Baratz, LMHC.
Description: New York, NY: Rodale, [2024] | Includes bibliographical references and index.
Identifiers: LCCN 2023049192 | ISBN 9780593581193 (hardcover) | ISBN 9780593581209 (ebook)
Subjects: LCSH: Love—Psychological aspects. | Interpersonal relations.
Classification: LCC BF575.L8 B237 2024 |
DDC 152.4/1—dc23/eng/20231218
LC record available at https://lccn.loc.gov/2023049192

Printed in the United States of America on acid-free paper

rodalebooks.com
randomhousebooks.com

1 2 3 4 5 6 7 8 9

First Edition

Book design by Susan Turner

*Dedicated to my mother
and my therapist, Derek—
my greatest teachers*

Contents

Introduction

Get Real

Your vision will become clear only when you can look into your own heart. . . . Who looks outside dreams; who looks inside awakes.

—CARL JUNG

What brought you here?

Let me guess: You picked up this book because you want change. You want to self-improve. And perhaps you're hoping this very book holds all the solutions you've been looking for.

You want your life to be better.

You want your relationship(s) to be better.

You want to have better sex.

You want to date better.

Better. Better. Better. Well, I want you to have better

everything, too. And I don't want you to feel like you're constantly about to lose your mind. So, I am here to help. But don't expect me to regurgitate the worn-out advice about self-love, attachment, or "true love" (whatever that even means). I will not be handing out another list of life hacks. None of that "Live, Laugh, Love" stuff. No ma'am.

Instead, I want to give you meaning. A story. Purpose. Community. Solidarity and connection. A deeper connection to yourself and to others. To me ☺.

And why? You need it. We all do.

Because . . . let me level with you: Life is a *wild* ride. It is a roller coaster of unpredictability and uncertainty. And love? Don't even get me started! Well, I'm actually just getting started. This is the intro!

Love will mess with your head in ways you'd never expect; you will lose your mind. I mean, think about it: The reality of adult love is that it is conditional, inherently uncertain, and fraught with risk. The idea of security is a total illusion. A literal mindfuck. Not to mention this cruel twist of fate: that we are unconsciously drawn to partners who mirror our unresolved issues from childhood.

We all unconsciously re-enact the past.

Some of us go further into these patterns, almost creating a second childhood. But can we be blamed for not knowing any different? Should we be criticizing ourselves for making these mistakes or having regrets? I'd say (emphatically) *no*-to-the-way.

We're all to some extent unhealthy. Like the weather, our relationships and overall emotional well-being are not always a sunshine state. Truly. You're bound to feel overwhelmed at times—as if a storm were raging inside you, pushing you to the brink of madness—only to wake up the next day to clear skies, as if nothing happened.

A life in love *will* at some point make you lose your mind. But it will also be your greatest teacher. It was and continues to be mine.

About six years ago, I ended my ten-year relationship with my partner Alex (more on him later), started dating (omfg!), and for the first time in my adult life experienced being single. Suffice it to say, I felt as if I were free-falling without a parachute. When my dates and casual sex partners started asking to connect with me on Instagram (apparently a prerequisite for dating these days), I created an account fast. (After all, how could I be a single person without social media?) Then I posted a selfie and some art, started following a few therapist influencers, and . . .

I was *shocked*.

Biggest gay gasp.

It was *madness*.

The information these so-called Insta-therapists and life coaches were peddling was nonsense. What they were telling people was totally incongruent with my experience in relationships, in therapy, as a therapist, and as a human being.

I saw a lot of overused buzzwords like *gaslighting, love bombing,* and *toxic* everything (and everyone). But it was the misinformation on codependency that brought me to action. According to the internet, any behavior with a hint of dependence was now under the microscope. Independence and autonomy were being presented as the gold standard of relationshipping. Insta-therapists offered up checklists of codependent behaviors without any contextualization or even a mention that *this might not apply to you.* My favorites were the listicles, the "10 Signs

You're Codependent"–type posts that included everything from "You're anxious if you don't hear from them" to "You'd prefer to spend time with your partner rather than be alone" to "You compromise and forgive too much."

Umm. Of course we might become anxious if we don't hear from a partner! And I don't know about you, but I definitely want to be in a relationship where I'd rather spend time with my partner than be alone. *Hello?* Isn't this why we form relationships in the first place?

That's not to say you shouldn't be able to or want to be alone sometimes. But the way dependency has been demonized is truly bewildering. All relationships, to some extent, are codependent. Think about Covid-19. If you lived with another person during 2020–21, you entered a codependent relationship!

But the codependency content online was just the tip of the iceberg. Large Insta accounts were posting diagnostic checklists that had been both oversimplified and wildly expanded. New labels ("people pleaser," "self-betrayal," "trauma bond," "higher and best self") proliferated, and traditional labels (narcissism, gaslighting, inner-child) were being applied far too broadly. I watched as the idea of addiction, for example, was expanded to the point where we can now be addicted to anything, even our own emotions.

I was astounded by the amount of posts I found that reframed normal relational problems as unhealthy. As if relationships weren't hard enough, now we have to contend with the idea that we have been "gaslit" by our partners, when we've actually been having simple, relationally healthy disagreements. Are our partners supposed to validate us all the time? No. They aren't, and they can't.

We are being gaslit by the content about gaslighting!

This was shocking to me. The most impactful aspect of my work as a therapist has centered on helping my clients feel comfortable in their own skin; helping individuals break down the limiting binaries and categories that were forced upon them by family and culture; helping couples stay together or separate with tremendous care. It has not been about helping clients find more ways to label themselves or their partners as toxic narcissists.

I wanted to help people embrace their humanity and normalize challenges. Yet, the more I read online, the more it seemed that mainstream thought was amplifying a trend of pathologizing and diagnosing others. Instead of medical diagnoses, we now have cultural diagnoses that label behaviors, thoughts, and emotions as "problematic" or "unhealthy" based on social norms, expectations, and prevailing trends.

People are selling sickness, and we're consuming it like hotcakes. This has left us in a state of panic, haunted by the idea that there is always something wrong with us or our relationships, always something that needs to be fixed and improved.

To combat this trend of oversimplified online "Insta-therapy," I decided to create my own content. My BFF, Lisa, and I brainstormed Instagram account names, and she came up with @yourdiagnonsense, from one of our favorite movies, *Girl, Interrupted*. (Thank you, @leethsa.) The handle made sense for me because so much about our culture's new pop psychology is diagnostic nonsense.

The initial content I shared on Instagram was rooted in my own experiences—past struggles of my own or stories from sessions with clients. As more Instagram users discovered my posts,

I started attracting couples and individuals to my practice, all of whom were grappling with issues that mirrored my own.

All my clients were around my age and either couples trying to work through conflict or individuals desperately trying to separate from or maintain stronger boundaries with family members. There was one client whose husband had cheated on her at the same time that my ex cheated on me. I even had a client whose father passed away at the same time as mine.

Being a therapist while going through major personal turmoil is a bizarre experience. And in this case, it seemed as if my clients and I were leading parallel lives—and we were. But not because of some great cosmic shift, or because Mercury was in retrograde, or my Virgo sun and moon were rising. No. The reason was simple: I, just like them, was a human being struggling to figure it all out in a culture that does absolutely nothing to help, a culture that, instead, teaches us how to feel shame about who we are and creates anxiety about living up to idealistic and unattainable standards.

As children, we spend more time learning how to do long division than how to identify our emotions, let alone how to communicate effectively. We don't thrive because of our capacity for mathematics. Our ongoing evolution has been, and will always be, based upon our shared humanity. The lack of social and relational guidance in our culture is outrageous at best and harmful to survival at worst.

The more I worked with individuals and couples on their relationships, the more I noticed the similarities in their stories. Everyone in my practice was relationally anxious, with *urgent* concerns about their relationships, but despite the uniqueness of each person, the underlying themes remained remarkably similar:

- Everyone has relational trauma that they re-enact within the context of dating or in intimate relationships (trauma they're *not* aware of and *yet* are anxious about).
- Everyone has unrealistic expectations about relationships and sex (expectations they're *not* aware of and *yet* are anxious about).
- Everyone feels shame for how they're experiencing their life, relationships, and sexuality (shame they are very much aware of and anxious about).

The new availability and access to information, satirical memes, and psycho-education on social media weren't helping ease my clients' distress. Instead, my patients were anxious, obsessed, and totally alone. Bombarded with self-help content. Spiraling. Analyzing. And totally paralyzed. With all the "experts" on social media, we as a culture seem to have been indoctrinated by a cultlike influence, and now we need to get deprogrammed to function peacefully.

How to start? Stop focusing on finding hard-and-fast guidelines for how you think you *should* be living your life. No more consulting top-ten lists for something that is highly nuanced and complex, something that cannot be adequately captured in a few bullet points. (And if you can't find the nuance and complexity, you're not looking hard enough.)

In short, we need a detox from the current rigid cultural dogma about love, sex, and life.

THE LOVE MARKETPLACE

Over the past few decades, Western culture has been setting the bar for personal fulfillment higher and higher, with love now expected to provide us with complete life satisfaction. I would argue that we are approaching love like yet another capitalist pursuit. The dating apps are essentially a marketplace, with potential partners the product being marketed and love as the highly sought-after luxury item.

Think about the dating process. Is it really that different from making a large purchase? You carefully weigh your options and consider a laundry list of factors, including social status, job, location, physical appearance, and perceived long-term compatibility (based on practically no information). Then you embark on a process of comparison, where one potential partner is compared to another as if you're choosing between two different products.

Simultaneously, we turn ourselves into marketable assets. We put our best foot forward to appeal to potential partners. This involves a calculated display of our attributes, similar to advertising a product.

We swipe to find a love interest who is beautiful, well-dressed, wealthy, ambitious, emotionally available, communicative. We want to have an exceptional partner, the happiest relationship, and the most passionate sex. We find someone who we think fits the bill and then, in the face of adversity, we automatically presume the worst. We begin a process of scrutiny where we obsess over every text message (or lack thereof) and misstep with our friends and trusted confidants.

We are pursuing a *marketed* version of love. You know what I'm talking about. Happily ever after. The fairy tale of the perfect match, the soulmate, or the one where it "all makes sense." An instantaneous and easy version of love that requires no effort with zero hurt.

When my single clients share their experiences while

dating, they often say, "I don't know if it's going to work because they _____."

I've Heard Everything:

"It's not going to work because he isn't free on Fridays."

"It's not going to work because they live in Brooklyn and I live on the Upper West Side."

"It's not going to work because she's a Gemini and I'm a Scorpio."

"It's not going to work because he has a child under the age of ten."

Everyone has a _____. And for them, there is a whole story as to why that _____ won't work. And it almost makes sense.

Rather than taking it slow—going on dates, really getting to know each other—we want to know with ease where it's going and how we're going to get there. We want an organic combustion of chemistry; a spark, fireworks. We all (even I sometimes) default to these "fantasies," but these givens are fundamentally false and unrealistic.

As our expectations for love have soared to unprecedented heights, our commitment to doing the necessary work to sustain that love has plummeted. This might be because we hold on to the fantasy that with the "right" person love will be total bliss. The truth is, every relationship will include unfulfilling and disappointing moments. This isn't necessarily an indicator of the wrong relationship or partner (though it could be). It's merely a reflection of the intricate nature of relationships themselves.

Maybe our belief in the fairy tale is what reassures us that the emotional risks and vulnerabilities we expose ourselves to in the pursuit of love will be worthwhile. But the fairy tale actually *sabotages* our relationships. And a more balanced strategy is within reach.

UNLEARNING "THE RULES"

The modern rules for love and life were set up for our protection. They act as defensive strategies. Born from a place of fear and anxiety, these defense mechanisms have now been rebranded as essential health measures to navigate relational experiences.

But I promise you there is a deeper story at play.

The new modern approach to love is about self-protection and safeguarding our independence. We're trying to protect ourselves in ways that prior generations did not or could not. And of course, we should. Most of us, at one point or another, have been devastated by someone or something. My grandparents were. My mother was. My father was. My brothers were. I never want to go back to that place (childhood), and I know you don't, either.

We are in the midst of a collective crisis, grappling with unresolved intergenerational traumas that persist in our present realities. Many of us come from families that have experienced significant traumas, which may have occurred not only within our immediate family but also prior generations. These unresolved traumas can be transmitted from one generation to the next, creating a cycle of suffering that persists over time.

Identifying red flags, maintaining boundaries, using labels, and avoiding all the narcissists we believe we've become experts at recognizing are actually normal trauma responses. Unfortunately, like most defense mechanisms, they can actually end up hurting more than helping. Instead of understanding, accepting, and/or tolerating the inevitable difficulties that arise in relationships, we may find ourselves condemning our partners, and even ourselves, for being imperfect.

I could say that all the rules and defense mechanisms are unhelpful, but it's not so black-and-white. There's value in setting standards to follow. If my mother had been more discerning with her choice of whom to spend the rest of her life with, or had felt that leaving was an option, she might not have stayed with an abusive partner (or chosen him in the first place). This would have been groundbreaking for my family, and I wouldn't have had a childhood defined by fear.

This isn't an all-or-nothing discussion; we *need* some rules to protect us from abusive partners and unsafe relationships.

However, *some* rules might not be applicable, or even necessary.

It's not that our expectations are too high. It's not that they're too low. It's that the focus is wrong. Mine. Yours. Theirs.

We need a *nuanced reframing.*

IT'S TIME TO GROW UP

The prevailing ideal for love is complete life fulfillment and acceptance. We anticipate that our partners will transform our lives for the better. Think about the enormity of this expectation: We are essentially designating our partners as our saviors.

I spent years hoping my ex would change so I could feel more satisfied. I was paralyzed, unable to ask for that change in a kind and productive way, and stuck in my thinking that my happiness *depended* upon his changing. But this is not how relational change works. And it wasn't love either; it was a rescue mission.

Here's the truth: *We change our relationships by changing ourselves.*

We would be better served to think about partnership first as a relationship with ourselves. Nope, this isn't about self-love. It is about self-understanding, self-awareness, and personal growth. The more self-aware and relationally minded we become, the better our chances of co-creating a fulfilling relationship, addressing challenges, and discerning when to walk away from relationships that no longer work.

And to change ourselves, we have to know how our history shapes our present and future fears. We have to become conscious of who we are, where we come from, and how we project those stories onto our partner(s).

This is the story I explore with my clients and this is the journey I've been on for twenty-five years with my own therapist, Derek.

This is a story about trauma and the unconscious mechanisms that permeate all our relationships. Our wounds hold the power to influence our choice of partners and the dynamics we eventually establish with them. This is what I will be referring to as re-enactments throughout the book. If you want to create safer relationships, taking responsibility for the role you play in creating these re-enactments is crucial. These re-enactments are about the collective traumas we inherit from our family's intergenerational stories.

Throughout this book, I'll invite you to embrace certain hard truths, particularly when it comes to navigating pain. I recognize that part of your motivation for picking up this book might have been to learn how to avoid these challenges. Instead, my goal is to empower you with confidence and inner strength, enabling you to confront the reality of our shared human condition.

This reality revolves around our fundamental predicament

in life—it's filled with challenges, moments of despair, and the inescapable presence of pain. Regrettably, we're often bombarded with messages that promise a life free from pain, portraying happiness as a constant and effortless state to attain. Our very efforts to avoid pain have created obstacles to well-being and overall life satisfaction.

If we are to truly grow, we must confront and accept our pain, even run toward it, and recognize that pain can be an invaluable teacher. Paradoxically, it is through facing and embracing these painful moments that we can experience significant personal growth and learn profound lessons about ourselves and our relationships.

In this book, you will delve deeply into the exploration of your unconscious psyche, and identify how your past informs your present. Together we will bring to light patterns and behaviors that may have lingered in the depths of your unconscious mind for too long. Don't worry. I don't expect you to be fully self-aware and healed in the time it takes to read this book. It's not something you have to do by next month or next year. These are things you will be doing throughout the rest of your life. They are to be done imperfectly over time. So, give yourself and everyone around you a big break.

Through each chapter, you'll be prompted to pause, reflect, and explore the depths of your emotions and experiences. It's not about rushing through the pages, but about immersing yourself in the narratives and insights presented and making meaningful connections to your own life.

The heart of this book lies not in providing answers but in helping you explore your own unique story and cultivate a greater understanding of the dynamics at play within your relationships. By becoming the author of your own story, you can start to reclaim your power and approach your life in a more intentional, mindful way.

This process requires patience. It's not about eradicating flaws or resolving all conflicts overnight, but about fostering compassion and kindness for yourself and others. It's about recognizing that love, life, and relationships are inherently complex, filled with joy and pain, successes and failures.

The purpose of reading this book is not to find a cure.

It's to find your story.

HOW TO LOVE SOMEONE
WITHOUT LOSING YOUR MIND

Emotional Ghosts

> Until we uncover the actual triggering event in our family history, we can relive fears and feelings that don't belong to us—unconscious fragments of a trauma—and we will think they're ours.
>
> —MARK WOLYNN, *It Didn't Start with You*

For over a decade, I've been working with individuals and couples, assisting them in exploring the narratives they create about love and life. Every challenge presented can be traced back to a sense of loss and an accompanying deep longing for love and acceptance.

Our experiences, including our emotions, desires, and challenges, are often felt as unique and isolated, seemingly disconnected from anything beyond ourselves, but we are not the starting point; instead, our lives are chapters within an older story that predates us. Therefore, a crucial aspect of the therapeutic process involves establishing a connection to this intergenerational narrative.

After a session with a client, it struck me that I possessed a greater understanding of my clients' parents' personal histories than I did about my own parents. This prompted me to have the same kind of in-depth conversations with my parents. If the option is available, I encourage you to conduct a similar interview with your parents. Read on for my mother's story, and in reading her interview, take note of the conversational style. At the end of this section, I share a number of questions to help you initiate your own interview with your parents.

INHERITED PAIN: MY PARENTS' STORY

"I just wanted to be loved."

That's what my mom said when I asked her why she chose to marry my father. She didn't say, "He fulfilled my needs" or "He validated my emotions." No mention of red flags or toxic behaviors (even though there were plenty). No discussion about similarities, differences, chemistry, soulmates, or theirs being the "right" match. None of the ways in which my clients and I talk about relationships. She just wanted love.

But what does love even mean? Of course, being a therapist, I wanted to know more. I continued. "What did love mean to you, Mom? What were you looking for in a partner before you met Dad?"

"Back then, love meant being admired," she said. "I wanted a guy who had a strong sense of family values, someone to take care of me and keep me safe."

No top-ten lists, no love languages, no attachment styles, criteria, or analysis required. Only admiration, family values, commitment, and caretaking.

"Is this what you learned from Nana?" I wanted to learn more about the context that informed my mother's ideas about love.

"I got married at twenty-two, and even then, my mother thought I was gay. They wanted you to marry at eighteen, twenty. And if you didn't, you were either gay, stupid, or ugly. I also wanted to escape my family, so this was the only way out I saw. I was taught that love meant finding someone who would marry you and have kids."

"Escape your family? What were you escaping?" I asked. I knew the basics of the story, but it felt like maybe she'd been holding back.

"Your father took me away from that home. From my stepfather. He would throw his food against the wall. It wasn't pleasant."

"So, he was abusive and violent?"

"You could say that. Yeah, he was abusive. Always angry. I hated when he would come home. I was scared of him. And then my mother would sit me down and tell me things she shouldn't have, because she had no one else to talk to. She would tell me about his flings. And she thought telling me would teach me a lesson about love and what to avoid."

I began to tear up. I'd known her stepfather was cold, but I hadn't known he was abusive. My father had also been abusive, and I was scared of him. My mother would often cry to me, telling me things she shouldn't have.

After the interview, I cried. I cried for her. I cried for myself. I cried for my clients. And I cried for you.

Your parents' stories are your stories. And if you're looking to build self-awareness, you may not get far without knowing more about the people who raised you. What's often so challenging is that most families don't talk about these things. They may even take it one step further and deny a history of trauma, or focus only on overly positive or idealistic memories. This brand of denial is common among trauma survivors. They use denial to protect themselves and their children from the horrors they were subjected to. Uncovering your family's hidden narratives is vital, as you might be unknowingly re-enacting them in your own life.

Before it's too late, make sure to take the time to ask the people who raised you about their life story. And if you have children, make sure you share yours with them. Not only is it a bonding experience, but I would even go as far as to say that it's necessary in order to heal your childhood wounds. It's often too simple to objectify and evaluate our parents based on our experience of being parented by them. However, it's essential to humanize and recognize them as complete individuals with stories of their own, much like ours. Knowing more about my mother's life gave me a powerful new perspective. I now understand why she did what she did. I understand how I inherited not just her brown eyes and thick hair but also her trauma. My father's story was just as full of upsetting patterns. When I interviewed him, he was much older and had developed early onset dementia. It was unclear which of his stories I could actually believe, but when I asked my mom, she confirmed that all were true.

My father's parents were born in the late 1890s, in a small town in Russian-controlled Ukraine before they fled and immigrated to the United States. (They were lucky to escape; many of their relatives were killed.) In the States, they struggled to make ends meet. They lived in South Boston and, after my father was born, Chelsea, Massachusetts. Both places were anti-Semitic, and my father was often targeted by neighborhood children; others drew swastikas on their front porch, or left broken glass in their driveway. My grandfather died when my father was eleven, and my grandmother tried to commit suicide right after. Tasked with taking care of his mother in her grief, my father was never able to fully express or experience his own. *Abandonment* doesn't begin to describe his experience of being a child. Once recovered, his mother had to work 24/7, but without childcare, she would leave him alone at the local movie theater for hours. He was just a kid. I was also often left alone as a child. And I was my mother's emotional caretaker.

Unfortunately, neither of my parents was able to recover from their childhood, and in adulthood, they would each unknowingly re-enact their unresolved issues. They grew up in a time when emotions, trauma, and violence weren't acknowledged. They weren't given the opportunity to heal, they didn't have anyone to talk to, and memes satirizing mental health certainly didn't yet exist.

In my family tree, after losing so many relatives due to war and the Holocaust, independence was discouraged to maintain the unity of the family structure; survival was the priority, not relational satisfaction or overall mental well-being. Further, being alone was associated with death, and as a result, everyone stayed in relationships despite them being abusive. I had interviewed my parents around the time I was contemplating the end of my relationship with Alex. I was ambivalent, paralyzed with fear in the face of ending a relationship with someone I

dearly loved and being alone. Without knowing it, I was working through the intergenerational story that my father, mother,
her mother, and prior generations had never been able to.

When you're preparing to interview your parents, it's crucial not only to arm yourself with productive questions (see the
sample questions that follow) but also to approach the conversation with sensitivity and without judgment.

Often, the depth and vulnerability of some questions
might lead us into unfamiliar territory, making the process
uncomfortable. I've heard this sentiment from my clients;
many of them express feelings of anxiety and confusion over
initiating such conversations with family members.

But there's meaning in such discomfort. That unease often
points toward a relationship dynamic built around avoidance
and denial. One of the most profound acts we can do in our
quest for personal growth is to disrupt these intergenerational
patterns of silence.

So, how do you kick off these chats? Just start. The words
you use to break the ice are yours. Maybe they'll be: "I recently
came across this amazing book (lol) that prompted me to
explore family histories." Or perhaps they'll be: "I found
myself reminiscing about Nana the other day, and I realized I
know so little about our family lineage and Nana's journey to
America. Would you share their story with me?" Whether it's
a crafted narrative or an organic inquiry, the key is to set the
ball rolling.

It's vital to remember that this is an interview, not an intervention. This isn't the setting in which to challenge or confront;
it's a space to listen and learn. Channel your inner Barbara
Walters, seeking the stories, the juicy details, and the family

gossip. If a comment or revelation catches you off guard, make a mental note of it and continue with grace. Approach the conversation with gentle kindness. If your parent or caregiver seems hesitant or guarded, gently push and redirect. Your aim? To bridge gaps, foster understanding, and deepen connections.

Sample Questions

- Can you tell me about your childhood home and the kind of environment you grew up in?
- What were the cultural norms or expectations about dating, love, relationships, and marriage while you were growing up?
- How has your perspective on love and relationships evolved over time?
- What can you tell me about your parents and the kind of relationship you shared with them?
- Do you have any cherished memories from your childhood that you can share?
- Are there any unpleasant or frightening memories from your childhood that you feel comfortable discussing?
- What were some of the challenges or difficulties you experienced while growing up?
- How would you describe your parents' relationship? Did they get along? How did they express affection? How did they resolve disagreements?
- What guidance or advice did your parents give you about dating, relationships, and intimacy? What were their expectations for your future relationships, such as the timing for marriage and children?
- Can you recall when you began dating? What were your experiences and how did they change over time?

- What were some qualities you valued in a partner?
- How did you strike a balance between pursuing your personal goals and nurturing your relationships?
- Could you share the story of how you met my other parent? Do you have any special memories from the early days of your relationship?
- What do you consider the biggest challenge in sustaining long-term relationships?
- If you had to give one piece of advice about love and relationships, what would it be?

A DECADE WITH ALEX

I was with Alex throughout all of my twenties. Ten years. We grew up together.

Sparks flew when we first met, so things moved quickly. I moved in after just four months. Part excitement, part an escape from my parents.

I had had long-term relationships before, but this was my first relationship where our lives were fully integrated. We had a life together, a house, a cute Havapoo named Zoey (aka ZZ, aka ZeeZoo), and a calendar of future travel. His family was mine, and my family was his.

It was *our* family.

I loved our life together, but as time went on, challenges arose. The only relationship I had with which to compare it was my parents', a total horror show. My father was abusive, and my mother had stayed with him because she was too afraid to be alone; she was threatened by the idea of her own independence and power.

Alex was definitely not abusive, and our relationship was fundamentally healthy, but I felt the same powerlessness and inability to own my voice that I had observed in my mother. When challenges arose with Alex, I was confronting more than the decision to leave or stay. It was about how I, like my mother before me, enacted anxious dependence and powerlessness in a relationship. She never demanded that my father go to therapy or get on meds. She never once called him abusive, even though we were all victims of his domestic violence. Instead, it was my mother, my three brothers, and I who all went to therapy and took meds.

I did the same thing. I never confronted Alex about his limitations or our relational challenges. Alex's limitations were not in any way similar to my father's, yet I responded to him the exact same way I responded to my father's mistreatment. I stayed small, quiet, and barely spoke. Even when I knew I was unsatisfied, I didn't push Alex for more. I asked him to go to therapy once. *Once!* Why didn't I ask more often? Because I was triggered, and I re-enacted the powerlessness I had learned from my family.

I spiraled in ambivalence for two years, curious about who else was out there but paralyzed by the prospect of losing someone whom I deeply loved. In short, I was having a second childhood. Stuck, powerless, and unable to leave, but also unwilling to try to make things work—even though, as an adult, I had power, independence, and all the tools necessary to either change the relationship or leave it.

I had no idea what I was doing. The only thing I knew was what I didn't want, and that was my parents' marriage.

Back Then, It Seemed I Had Two Options:
1. Stay in the relationship with Alex and remain unsatisfied.
2. End the relationship and find another partner (lol, as if it's that easy).

What Was Missing Was a Third Option:
3. Work on the relationship as fucking hard as I possibly could and, if it didn't work, end it and learn how to be on my own.

I went with option one until I couldn't bear it any longer. Looking back on it all now, I see that I never even gave option three a chance. Most people don't.

Eventually, I did end my relationship, and it was excruciating. I was in a state of grief for years. (It still pops up.) I was lost for a long time, rebuilding my life and trying to find myself.

Part of me is still searching, still building.

YOU ARE NEVER TRAPPED, AND IT IS NOT HOPELESS

Whether you are single, in a relationship, or going through a gut-wrenching breakup, whatever you seek *is* attainable. You *can* make changes and achieve what you want (or something close to it). I'm not saying you'll have a problem-free life. (Give up that hope ASAP.) Instead, you'll have the freedom to make better decisions that lead to a more *satisfying* and *meaningful*, although still *imperfect*, life.

Change toward self-acceptance.

Change toward the ability to laugh at your own shit instead of condemning yourself or blaming those you love.

Change toward mind-blowing orgasms.

Do I have the answers for how you should be living your life? Not exactly. But you do. And I'm going to help you find them. This is your power, and I want you to own it. Chances are, it was once taken from you. My hope is that this book will help you find it again.

This is the emotional and relational curriculum you didn't learn in school.

Buckle up. School is now in session.

Modern Love Is a *Mess*

In love, happiness is an abnormal state.

—MARCEL PROUST

People date with the goal of finding their perfect match, "the One." We want someone special. Someone whose genitals are the perfect mirror to ours—like two puzzle pieces fitting together seamlessly. Like lightning striking—boom! Cue the symphony to emphasize perfect bliss (and multiple orgasms).

Oh, and of course, lest we forget, "the One" must also be 100 percent emotionally available, stable, healed, therapized, able to communicate. They must be motivated, funny, growth-oriented, mature. With a good job and impeccable taste. They must love travel and dogs. Be in shape and a foodie, with no imperfections, no red flags—just chemistry, connection, and love at first sight. Oy vey!

STOP LOOKING FOR "THE ONE"

I know I said we were throwing out the rules, but here's a rule you can keep in your back pocket: Stop looking for the One.

Everyone goes on dates armed with a list of needs, desires, and expectations. We know what we want in a partner with regard to their height, weight, career, and clothing style. Why are we doing this? Because we believe that this will allow us to build the best relationship with the least amount of difficulty and pain. Unfortunately, this kind of curated search for love makes it impossible for us to truly connect.

The current culture around dating is a mess, a real problem. Most people approach dating without any information about how to develop a relationship. Instead, their focus is on seeking excitement, chemistry, or "the spark." The One. It's why more and more people have become avoidant, distant, and deeply alone. Many others have become resolute in their single lives, declaring that they don't need a partner to complete them.

Dating in today's world presents a unique set of challenges that were absent for past generations. We now have online dating, with myriad apps promising love or, at the very least, a connection. Each platform presents the same pool of singles within a fifty-mile radius, all available at the swipe of a finger. A simple swipe, tap, or "like" has become the new way of saying, "You're hot."

But with these advancements have come setbacks. The

heartbreak of being ignored, left on "Read," or ghosted is all too familiar. Then there are the dates that go awry, where you find that the person sitting across from you hardly resembles their curated online photos. Perhaps they have body odor, or bad breath, or make odd noises that weren't apparent over text. But perhaps the most disheartening of all? Engaging in wonderful conversations that span days, or even weeks, feeling a genuine connection, only to be met with silence, never hearing from the person again.

This is dating today. It can be wildly exhausting and devoid of hope, yet it is a necessary evil if you're looking for something meaningful. Kind of like eating when you're not hungry: You just have to do it.

Most people who are on the dating treadmill end up fearful, guarded, and cold. They are freaked out about their value, the possibility of rejection, and generally anxious. This translates into the exact opposite of chemistry: disconnection. So, how can we expect to show up on yet another first date and be 100 percent ourselves? It's just not going to happen.

RELATIONSHIPS ARE BUILT

If you are single, dating, and deeply trying to find someone capable of commitment, focus on simply showing up, listening, and learning about the other person. Ask yourself if you're having fun. Put your effort into actually getting to know someone and letting them get to know you.

During the early stages of dating, the time spent together and the communication should be consistent and reliable. For some, this means dinner once a week or once a month. You decide with your new/ potential partner. Similarly, when it comes to texting, some people want constant communication and banter (I do), and some don't. Again, you decide this with your partner. And if you're confused about what's next, you must ask. Always. There is nothing wrong with asking. Do not withdraw.

Relationships are built, not manifested. Put effort into the building. Create that solid foundation. Stop looking for red flags, psychoanalyzing the other person, or making assumptions based on the limited information you have thus far collected. Get curious and be creative! Go on dates and ask meaningful questions. Go on adventures and have new experiences.

During the first few dates, people often experience heightened anxiety. These initial encounters are defined by assumptions about the other person based on a dating profile or an Instagram feed. Being present has been replaced with one part intellectual analysis and two parts urgent hypervigilance. The result? Instead of being present on that first date, really listening and learning, we're on high alert, trying to decipher how much the other person sitting across from us will one day hurt us. I call this the *hurt potential*. The hurt potential is a future-focused process defined by the "what-ifs."

"What if we're incompatible because they like to go out and I'm a homebody?"

"Is it a red flag if they still talk to their ex? What if they
    haven't moved on?"
"What if they judge me for struggling at work? I will focus on
    the positive."
"What if they're not family oriented? They said they don't
    have a close relationship with theirs . . ."

Translation: "What if _____ is a problem, and I get
hurt?" This is not what it means to be present; this is what it
means to be fearful. The result? A lack of vulnerability and an
increase in levels of the stress hormones cortisol and adrenaline, which will prevent you from being present.

Now imagine that you have finally found your "knight in
shining armor." You've determined that, with this person, the
potential for love outweighs the potential for hurt. Well, get ready,
because at some point down the line, the honeymoon phase will
end, and the person you put up on that pedestal will massively
disappoint you. Then, suddenly, your once-hopeful expectations
will warp into an ugly combination of resentment and contempt.

By no means am I discouraging expectations, dreams, or
desires for your future or current boo. Have them. Dream and
fantasize. But be sure to make a big distinction between your
dreams and the reality of life and love.

Let me break it down for you. We each carry a set of relationship rules that are shaped and defined by our culture and
religion. They tell us how to proceed with our relationships,
including everything from talking to an ex to opinions about
age differences as well as determining the timing of moving in
together, getting married, and starting a family. We internalize
these guidelines as absolute truths, using them as our guiding
compass in life to protect our hearts.

However, here's the catch: These rules and cultural norms aren't based on concrete facts, nor are they universally applicable. They are products of their respective times, and they have evolved over the years. That's why I shared my mother's story with you and encouraged you to explore your own family's experiences. Rules are essentially societal values, and they change as our culture changes. I would even go so far as to say . . .

CULTURE DEFINES LOVE

The tapestry of love and marriage has a complex history that has been shaped by cultural, economic, and social factors.

Historically, the very concept of love in marriage was considered an unaffordable luxury. Instead, the focus was on a suitable marriage, with or without love. For centuries, marriage was a matter of practicality, financial security, and social positioning—it was less about romance and more about connecting for the couple's mutual benefit.

Fast-forward to today, and you'll see that the concept of love has undergone a complete and total paradigm shift. We pursue a love that fulfills our dreams without infringing upon our freedoms. We yearn for a love that promises perpetual happiness, unwavering support, and lifelong companionship—with a partner who is also a confidant, co-parent, best friend, sous chef, and yes, even a dog walker. We set our sights on nothing short of exceptional love because, deep down, we believe our self-worth depends upon it. A union that was once based on the unconditional sentiment of "till death do us part" is now shifted to something more conditional, based on overall satisfaction and fulfillment.

But when my mother met my father in the 1960s, the rules

for love were very different. One rule my mother followed was to get married and have kids. Another rule was to stay in the marriage no matter what. Stay for the kids. Stay because you can't be a single woman at fifty; no one will want you. My mother wasn't taught about abuse or trauma. She didn't even know how to label the domestic violence she grew up with until I reframed it for her decades later. Her primary focus was on finding security and stability through marriage.

This was a culture of denial, and it prevented generations from confronting and healing their family trauma. But it wasn't merely a matter of individual denial; it was a societal and cultural dismissal of these issues in their entirety.

Fortunately, our understanding of trauma has deepened, highlighting the need, and making way, for new cultural rules. These are essential for safeguarding us and ensuring that future generations don't face similar hardships.

So, yes, rules about abuse are good and necessary. Safety is the most important part of a relationship. Expectations about being treated with kindness and empathy should be a given. However, rules about getting constant validation from a partner or being honest 100 percent of the time, for example, are unnecessary for safe and satisfying relationships. The pendulum has swung too far in the other direction. Prior generations had few rules for emotional protection. Now we have an entire encyclopedia of them!

I know what you might be thinking. "I want these rules. I don't see anything wrong with them. I want to be validated, I want to have a partner where it will be 50/50, I want a partner to be my better half." But I want you to understand that that checklist can't be the primary compass for navigating dating and relationships. Let them be soft *guidelines;* your primary goal is to be present and connect.

If you let some of the current rules drive the bus, I guarantee you, they will sabotage your relationship. You'll find yourself seeing your partner not as a separate individual with a unique history and unique needs, but rather in terms of what they can provide for you. This mindset will be a barrier to your truly connecting and resolving the deeper issues that will inevitably emerge in your relationship.

Love is about valuing a person, not their utility. We have to stop viewing potential partners through the lens of what they can "provide" or "offer" us and, instead, cherish who they are as individuals.

This is what happened with my client Eric.

ERIC: CAREGIVING AS A DESIRE TO BE CARED FOR

Eric is a client I've seen for years. He is a forty-three-year-old heterosexual cis-male from the Middle East. His origins trace back to Israel, the country from which he emigrated two decades ago at the age of twenty for his undergraduate studies. He entered therapy reporting feelings of deep loneliness and anxiety over not being able to find a partner.

Over the following six months, I learned about his childhood. Eric was incredibly close with his parents but often played the role of a caretaker. This is what therapists working with clients who've experienced a variety of trauma would call false empowerment, parentification, or emotional abandonment. Take your pick. In each of these instances, the caregiver's preoccupation with their own emotional needs leads to the neglect

and/or deprioritization of the child's needs. Eric's mother struggled with anxiety, and he became her go-to source of comfort,
her security blanket in a world teeming with uncertainty. His
father, on the other hand, was like a peripheral character in the
story of his life, often working, disengaging in front of the TV,
or secluding himself in his bedroom. His parents were Russian
immigrants who had relocated to Israel just prior to Eric's birth.
This move was challenging for the family, as the immigration
process placed the burden of responsibility on Eric's parents to
also facilitate their own parents' (Eric's grandparents') transition
to a new country. The obligation of caregiving in their family
spanned generations.

Yet Eric's mother was his companion, and her presence
was important to him even if it meant she was emotionally
unavailable and he was the one doing the parenting. Playing
certain roles in a family to receive love, approval, and affection
or keep the peace is a common family dynamic and an adaptive stance for the child who needs to maintain a connection in
order to reinforce a sense of safety and security. At the core of
this complex dynamic is a deep desire to connect, belong, and,
ultimately, be loved. Unfortunately, Eric's need to be taken
care of came second.

At the beginning of therapy, Eric was protective of his
mother in his accounts of the past and present. It took me
a few months to get him to confront, on an intellectual level,
that there were things he wanted that his parents hadn't given
him. Many people enact an unconscious loyalty to their families, often refraining from acknowledging negative sentiments
or past grievances. This reflects a deep-seated desire to protect and maintain family connections. But it also requires us

to suppress our own emotional experience and any specific unfulfilled desires.

The Russian culture in which Eric grew up placed significant value on respect for one's elders. The emphasis on respect for older generations is not a simple practice but a deeply ingrained value held by diverse cultures worldwide. At a young age, Eric was taught never to challenge or question the actions or views of his parents and grandparents. Consequently, reflecting on the potential harm they might inadvertently have caused him became difficult, as he had never been empowered or given permission to pursue such an idea.

I always ask my clients about their parents and grand-parents. When I inquired about Eric's mother's past, it became clear that she had experienced a form of emotional abandonment by her own parents. She had been raised in a home where her brother had a profoundly debilitating case of multiple sclerosis. Consequently, she found herself retreating and taking on the role of a helper to her own mother, much as Eric was doing now for her. The role, one could say, had been passed down from one generation to the next. Understanding Eric's history with caretaking was essential in order to fully comprehend what would emerge in his next romantic relationship.

He was dating and feeling increasingly hopeless. He went through a long string of first dates but failed to connect with any of the women he met. Naturally, he fell into the common trap of presuming he was doomed to eternal solitude. Alone forever.

Like most people entering the dating pool, Eric had a mental checklist of qualities he desired in a partner, a list I consistently reframed as anxiety and encouraged him to reconsider.

He was picky in the extreme, and my attempts to soften his rigid criteria became a recurring theme in our sessions. To challenge his obsessive focus on the unknown and reframe his anxiety, I adopted a simple, humorous strategy: I would firmly yet playfully say, "Stop it." I find myself repeating this phrase quite often with clients, to be honest. It might not be the most conventional therapeutic approach, but when it's delivered in a lighthearted manner, my clients (including Eric) seem to appreciate the humor in it. This is not meant to disregard or minimize the object of someone's obsession but rather to emphasize the importance of recognizing hypervigilance as anxiety and redirecting their focus toward the underlying meaning of that anxiety.

Luckily, he stopped. Aaaaand . . . enter Julia! ☺

Eric met Julia, and the two quickly hit it off. Over the course of the year, they grew closer and decided to move in together and settle down. I was thrilled, Eric was thrilled, they were thrilled.

Initially, Julia's daily presence provided Eric with a sense of lightness, fun, and relief from his anxiety. However, as their relationship progressed (and their intimacy grew), Eric began to focus on their differences and Julia's perceived limitations. Soon after they had moved in together, it became apparent that Julia was a neat freak, easily distracted, and absorbed in her own world. Her world was full of anxiety, rigid rules about free time, and a preference for relaxing activities that didn't necessarily involve connecting with Eric. Julia would have outbursts of frustration and anxiety over normal, everyday stressors. Without even realizing it, Eric shifted back into caretaker mode, re-enacting with Julia the role he had taken on with his mother: He became her caretaker and, in the process, deprioritized his own needs.

It wasn't just that Julia was taking up too much emotional space (though she was), it was also that Eric was giving that space to her, leaving himself very little. Instead of taking emotional space for himself, he would wait for Julia to give it to him—which, unfortunately, never happened. This only reinforced Eric's growing negative view of her. He created narratives about her character, gradually reshaping his perspective on who she was. To him, Julia was now selfish, self-involved, and lacking in empathy. And it was into this observation that Eric retreated farther. The loneliness he had once experienced while dating was now mirrored within his relationship, leaving him feeling adrift and emotionally abandoned by his partner— not unlike his experience in childhood.

Eric always brought coffee to session and would nervously sip on it. I'd always remind him that caffeine exacerbates anxiety, but as many of us do, we ignore that advice for the jolt of energy. One day, Eric came, coffee in hand, plopped himself on the couch, and dove right in. (Side note: I *love* it when clients dive right in.)

ERIC: I can't take it anymore. I don't think Julia has the capacity for empathy, or maybe it's just that she is so anxious and preoccupied with herself that she forgets I am even there. And when I bring it up, it seems like she isn't listening.

ME: No empathy? Like, *none*? That sounds kind of awful. Tell me, how often and when?

ERIC: I don't know, maybe once a week. If I tell her I don't like her being on her phone when we're watching TV together, she usually responds with a defensive statement about why she did it, rather than tending to my concern. And then she picks up her phone again! You'd think she would come over to me and give me a kiss or show me some kind of affection. Or, bare minimum, put the phone down! This is how it always goes.

Now, I know you might be thinking, *She's on her phone. What's the big deal?* Or, contrastingly, *How rude.* I was thinking both. But I also knew that it wasn't about the phone: Eric felt comfortable only when making the phone the center of the conversation (being critical of Julia), instead of expressing his desire to connect and get the attention (love) he sought. This was the dynamic he and Julia had co-created; these were the roles they'd taken on—Eric as the caregiver and Julia as the one being cared for. Eric began to resent Julia because he was always looking after her. Every time Julia made a mistake, or didn't meet his expectations, it became another piece of evidence for him that she wasn't able to meet his needs as a partner.

What I haven't mentioned yet is that Eric and Julia have a wonderful life together! Eric has fun when they go out. He loves staying in and cooking with her. After moving in together, they both had fun unpacking and decorating their new home. And Eric loves Julia's family.

I jumped back in.

ME: Whoa! Okay, this sounds lonely, and I can definitely see why you are upset. I'm not sure it's necessarily about the phone. The phone is a metaphor. Let's think a little more on this without condemning Julia. Because Julia can be flawed *and* still be a good partner for you. (She is both.) What I'm struck by most is how familiar this dynamic sounds. It's a direct parallel to the role you played with your mother. You had to take care of your mother's anxiety—just as you do with Julia—and as a result, you were not able to ask for special caretaking. Children have developmental needs for certain types of caretaking, which you unfortunately missed out on. And we can think of this as emotional abandonment.

Eric was silent. He crossed his legs and shifted his gaze downward.

Sometimes I'll pause a session to address my observations of noticeable changes in body language. I check in and say a therapisty thing like "I noticed your face just sank. You crossed your legs. You folded your arms. What's happening?" But this time I kept going, because I knew exactly what was happening: I had hit a wound Eric didn't want to deal with. Whenever I brought up his mother, I was met with opposition. So, of course, I brought her up often.

Me: I want to emphasize that it's not my responsibility to determine how much invalidation or challenge you can or should tolerate in your relationship. Everybody is different, and some may find a level of challenge to be too much, leading them to feel unseen and triggered. Or you may be able to manage these challenges. In your case, Eric, I want you to know that based on what you've shared the moments of invalidation and challenge you face are not the majority of your relationship with Julia. You both have fun together, go on trips, and you have reported feeling generally satisfied with your life together. Right?

As I was addressing these points, I noticed a subtle change in Eric's demeanor. His body tightened, and he seemed like he was about to check out. This was in the summer, and the hum of the air-conditioning in the background seemed to grow louder within the silence as I waited for a response from him.

Finally, Eric sighed heavily, breaking the silence. His voice quavered a bit, demonstrating his internal struggle. His eyes finally met mine.

ERIC: I see what you mean. It's just . . . I don't know how to . . . change my approach. It's . . . hard. And to be honest, I think it's hopeless. Things aren't going to change. There is nothing I can do to make her change. Plus, I'm angry!

I nodded, acknowledging his struggle.

ME: Indeed, Eric, change is incredibly challenging! Relationships aren't easy-breezy. They stir up everything. And Julia definitely has issues. And those issues have stirred up your issues.

I continued:

ME: Let's think more about this. You've never been able to participate in an intimate relationship where you prioritized your own needs, emotional experiences, and other preferences over your partner's. Instead, you prioritize others'. You learned this way of being during childhood, in your family, and you have re-enacted this familiar role in most if not all of your relationships. Which is definitely a positive attribute and what makes you such a good partner. And it just so happens that you chose an anxious partner who would require you to become a caretaker. There is something powerful here for you. You were never able to truly confront your mother or prioritize your own needs. You *can* do this with Julia, but you can't do so with the same longing for Julia to fulfill your needs that you had as a kid toward your mother. Julia is not your mother, and you can let her be anxious without having to take care of her. You can let her be anxious without deprioritizing your voice. This is the role you play, and it isn't about blame. It's about history, context, and dynamics. It's essential to accept that you can want more from your relationship while also understanding that it's okay to not always get what you want—unlike in childhood, when not getting your needs met had a lifelong impact. You wanted attention then, and you want attention now. And I think you can get it. But you will have to let go of your expectations and change your approach.

Throughout our sessions, Eric and I addressed a variety of other conflicts. The most significant obstacle for him, me, and possibly you is to understand how to identify triggers from our childhood and the anxiety that arises from expectations surrounding love and relationships. These two factors intersect and reflect a larger cultural issue beyond choosing the wrong partner.

When looking for love, we create lists of qualities we seek in a partner. We feel entitled to constant validation. We want our partners to make us a priority, even when we fail to do the same for ourselves. We expect our partners to satisfy all our needs, and every one of their missteps triggers anxiety. We expect our partner to change the habits, behaviors, or personality traits we find inconvenient or irritating—just because we told them to (once or twice). We want constant attention from our partner, viewing their dedication to any other interest or personal challenge as a sign of uninterest in us.

While totally reasonable wishes, these are all unrealistic expectations. The largeness of the emotion driving us to get our needs fulfilled often mirrors the pain we experienced in early childhood, when those needs weren't met. But as adults, in mature relationships, we don't actually need these things, especially not from our partners. I know as well as you how easy it is to become fixated on a specific trait or limitation in a partner while discounting the contexts and dynamics that created that trait or limitation in the first place.

While in session, to develop a more nuanced and complex understanding (without judgment, of course) of my clients' lives, I help my clients (as I did Eric) unravel the psychological and cultural contexts that shape their experience. Deepened self-awareness drives change and personal growth. But personal growth is about more than just gathering information or gaining insight; it's about training ourselves to shift from judgment to understanding. When we judge, we limit our potential for growth. Conversely, when we refrain from judgment, create a meaningful narrative, and appreciate complexity, we open ourselves up to more opportunities for personal development and self-improvement.

Context is everything. Don't ignore the bigger picture. Context is the who, what, when, where, and why of your life.

Think of context—or your life—as a garden. Everything influences how that garden flourishes. Just as the atmosphere and soil play a role in the garden's growth, every detail of your life contributes to shaping who you are.

Factors like where you were raised, family dynamics, and finances all play a part. Your identity (think gender, race, ethnicity, and culture of origin) mediates how everything in your life develops. Challenges like health issues or even just a lack of sleep can drastically affect your well-being and relationships. So, just as in a garden, where each element has a purpose and consequences, in life literally everything matters.

Few of us approach our lives and relationships with such an expansive understanding, but doing so is crucial. This is particularly relevant when considering how profoundly marginalized groups like BIPOC (Black, Indigenous, and other People of Color), LGBTQ+, and those with disabilities experience their lives. These folks frequently navigate complex layers of challenges. Racism, homophobia, transphobia, sexism, and ableism continue to exist in most environments across the world. These hostile spaces destroy one's feelings of self-worth. Lacking a feeling of acceptance and safety will influence all aspects of life, from one's relationships and sex life to one's career trajectory. These doubts and fears rest beneath the surface of our conscious understanding, where they quietly, yet powerfully, shape our lives in ways we may not always notice.

We each bring to the table our unique histories, contexts, and varied needs in our relationships. These elements connect to everything in our lives, from childhood traumas to toxic cultural value systems and beyond. Seek out these nuances and complexities that define your relationship. Embrace the layers of the unknown and buckle up for the ride. This is part of what makes life satisfying and, yes, a bit scary, too.

As you follow along in my narrative and those of my clients, begin applying these insights to your past, present, and future relationships. Start rebuilding and reshaping your relational guidelines. This process may seem daunting, but trust me, it's a rewarding endeavor that will make your life and love all the more enriching.

The Story

The past is never dead. It's not even past.
—WILLIAM FAULKNER, *Requiem for a Nun*

LIFE BEFORE ALEX

Before I tell you about Alex, you need a little background on me, my family, and the world that seemed to be preparing me for him—not in a manifested, "woo-woo" way, but in there being a void that defined my internal world and the type of love for which I unconsciously, desperately hungered. Let's go back to the beginning.

I grew up at the tail end of the 1980s and '90s in Newton, Massachusetts, an affluent, liberal, Jewish suburb about twenty minutes outside Boston. My home was a scary one, with fighting, sadness, anger, and a lot of pain on repeat.

I came out as gay when I was fourteen. Actually, I was outed by one of my three older brothers when he read my journal. When I asked him why he had outed me, he said he was trying to "protect" me from my homophobic and abusive father. Needless to say, this backfired; in my family, we were all adversaries. My parents handled it terribly. My father told me I was wrong and claimed it was a phase. My mother just cried.

Queerness, or gayness, was an unacknowledged reality in my family and overall community then. While Newton was pretty liberal, and my high school had a Gay-Straight Alliance, it was the '90s, and being gay was definitely *not* cool. The only information I had about what it meant to be gay was either from my mom's hairstylist or from *Will and Grace* and *Queer as Folk*. With the lack of queer visibility, I knew only of the supposed consequences of being gay: HIV/AIDS, drug use, and perpetual loneliness. At the time, being gay also represented loss. It meant I wasn't ever going to get married or have children or even experience long-term companionship.

All three of my brothers worked for my parents. But working in the family business, while lucrative, was not an emotional privilege. It was merely an extension of the warfare at home transferred to an office setting. My father would play favorites, pit everyone against one another, and bark harsh criticisms at my brothers for normal mistakes or simply for being there. And my mother co-signed my father's bullshit by doing nothing.

Abuse was trickle-down economics in my family. My brothers were hurting, and no one helped them or showed them compassion. As a result, their treating me with kindness was off the table. I would often cry to them about how mean and crazy our father was. The line they used on repeat was "We all had to go through it. Now it's your turn."

As I write this, I haven't spoken to my brothers in years. We are estranged. It's important to note that siblings can have completely different experiences within the same family. This can be a result of a variety of factors, from personality, to age difference, to individual relationship with one's parents, to birth order and the roles and responsibilities each is given within the family. For example, as the youngest, I was never tasked with being responsible for my brothers, whereas my eldest brother was responsible for me and my three other brothers from a very young age. It was completely unfair to him and a recipe for creating resentment, even hatred, in him—which is what happened.

While my family was majorly dysfunctional, every one of us spent time in psychotherapy (with questionable results). So, naturally, when I started experiencing emotional challenges at age ten, I was put into therapy. But it wasn't until I was fifteen that I formed the most important relationship in my life—with a therapist named Derek. I still see him today. It's one of the longest and most meaningful relationships I've ever had. It's been over twenty years.

Derek always said, "Don't let your family define you."

After years of messaging from my family about how needy, problematic, and unstable I was, I, too, had invested in my own incompetence.

We all internalize the messages, stories, values, and rules we learn from our family. James Hollis, an American psychoanalyst, put it well when he spoke about how we internalize the stories of the outside world. He said, "I am as I am treated."

Pause. Read that again out loud.

"I am as I am treated."

Put the book down (just for one second).

Now close your eyes and connect to an experience in which you internalized the way you were treated, whether it be from childhood or in your adult life. Maybe it's something related to your identity (think race, gender, ethnicity, etc.). Feel something about who you are. About your context.

Okay. Pick up the book again.

I started planning my escape from home to New York City the year I was outed. As one of the queerest cities in the country, New York was a liberating and empowering experience for me. It's where I found respite from an abusive family. New York symbolized freedom and safety.

I went to the Gallatin School of Individualized Study at NYU, which meant I could create my own major. It was life-changing. I blended psychology, medical philosophy, anthropology, and sociology to learn not only about the psychological classification of human experience but also about how culture shapes and defines how we experience reality in the first place. This has been one of the biggest influences upon how I currently practice as a therapist. Unfortunately, while my mind was being blown in class (and I was blowing guys), emotionally, I was struggling.

My family had never supported my desire to go to college—they'd wanted me to work in the family business—and they did everything they could to get in the way of my education. At one point, they stopped paying my tuition and refused to send me money for food. There was also that six-month period when they didn't pay my rent—not because I was doing poorly in school (I had a 4.0 GPA), and not because they didn't have the money (they had plenty), but because, having never gone to college themselves or never having been encouraged or allowed to by their parents, they did not value education and resented having to pay for mine.

But I got through all this thanks to Derek. During this time, it was Derek who sent me money for food. It was Derek who texted me daily and served as my surrogate parent. Some people thought this was inappropriate, judgment I was used to.

Something similar had happened when I was a teenager: My parents stopped paying for therapy after I came out because my father blamed Derek for "making me gay." During what I thought was to be our last session, Derek said, "Do you think I'm going to just stop seeing you?"

I remember it like it was yesterday, because it was one of the biggest turning points in my life. I thought, *Yes, of course.*

But Derek said no, and we continued for decades without me paying.

So, yes, Derek saved my life. Through decades of darkness, he taught me what it meant to be resilient. He has been the main figure in my life, the person who has protected me from spiraling into the psychosis that was almost guaranteed me by my family. Everyone should have a figure in their life like Derek—someone to go to for empathy, unconditional support, and love. If you're lucky, that person is one or both of your parents. But for many people, that's just not the reality.

My parents eventually caved and restarted the tuition payments, but it was with Derek's emotional support that I was able to finish college. Unfortunately, I finished in 2008, during the financial crisis. My bachelor's degree in the cultural construction of psychology wasn't getting me jobs. Out of options, I relocated to Boca Raton, Florida, the place my parents had lived for decades.

Florida was supposed to be a pit stop for me: I would move there temporarily while applying to grad schools. Derek and I strategized our timetables and coordinated on application deadlines and program start dates. It was the artificial light at the end of the tunnel, but we both knew it was a disaster waiting to happen. Leaving New York City to live with my parents was probably the worst thing for my mental health.

My father was a raging narcissist and fully physically disabled my entire life. The year I was born, he lost his vision, developed peripheral neuropathy (numbness in the hands and feet), and physically decompensated to the point where he couldn't walk. Throughout my life, he required a kidney transplant, experienced two heart attacks and three strokes, had to have a pacemaker and a defibrillator implanted, and had toes amputated due to his diabetes. He seemed bionic. I'm probably forgetting all his ailments, but let's just say he was very sick and that he stayed very sick until he died. He truly had a terrible existence—and his mood was just as miserable and overrun by illness as his body. None of us were close with him, as he was verbally and physically abusive toward everyone in the family.

So, going back to live under the same roof with my father was scary, to say the least.

As for my mother, I was, and still am, very close with my mother, a case study in herself.

My mom was raised in the 1940s. As I wrote earlier, she believed that her purpose was to get married. Discouraged from obtaining an education, she went from living with an abusive mother and stepfather to living with an abusive husband, organizing her life around being of service to him and her children at all costs—even abuse. And she was greatly underappreciated. (I never would have known all this if I hadn't sat her down for the interview I shared with you earlier.)

My mom was my father's nurse, cook, and babysitter. She would spend her days trying to please this unhappy, ragefilled man by making the foods he claimed to love: borscht, kreplach (meat dumplings), a variety of mayo salads (think chicken salad, tuna salad, and chopped liver), and ham sandwiches on Wonder Bread. (With my father being diabetic, this was the absolute worst food he could have eaten.) Food was the only thing they really had left. Yet, nothing seemed to satisfy him, though she kept trying—an apt analogy for their fiftyyear marriage.

So, naturally I was scared to go live with them down in Florida, but I'd exhausted all other options. Living there was as awful as I expected. If he wasn't verbally attacking my mother, my father was honing in on me as his next target. Not surprisingly, he employed the same tactics he had used when I was a teenager: laying down arbitrary rules about using the car (he didn't want me using *his* car, in case he needed it; mind you, he didn't have a driver's license because he was legally blind); questioning the amount of time I spent in the shower; questioning (criticizing) me for shaving my body; questioning (criticizing) my body in general; guilting me for living rent-free and not working in the family business; and expressing concern (criticism) for my eating too much, for not eating enough, for speaking too softly, for not speaking enough, for speaking too much. But, of course, I was used to this type of treatment from him. By that point, my dissociation and withdrawal were an automatic reflex.

Yet, somehow, my returning to this abusive environment as a horny twenty-one-year-old did not kill my libido.

You should know that stress and anxiety are directly linked to all things sexual. For some people, their libido increases when experiencing stress or anxiety and for others it decreases. Many people discount the role of stress (or any other emotional experience, for that matter) in sexual functioning, yet it is actually our emotions and accompanying hormones that regulate our sexual expression. Sex is yet another experience we all need to learn how to contextualize. (Don't worry, we will get to that.)

Jerking off was my escape. (Cue people judging the use of masturbation for self-soothing and pleasure.) Just so it's clear: Masturbation is a wonderful coping mechanism for emotional or physical pain. Do it as much as you want. Derek is also a sex therapist, and we talked early on about the importance of masturbation. Masturbation is a central feature of sexual health. Yet because many people do not get the experience of empowerment early on, they struggle to access this invaluable internal resource.

While masturbation was great, what I really wanted, craved, was the touch of someone else (and someone else's dick). I had no friends in Florida, so I figured casual sex could be a way to meet someone. So, I went on adam4adam.com (a hookup website, as apps weren't around yet). It was there, on that sex website, that my whole life would completely change.

That's where I met Alex.

When I first saw him, I thought, *Cute.* But I was on autopilot

and sought "NSA" (that's "no strings attached") casual sex—
something I enjoyed then. The expectation was to have "fun"
and get off. Back then, my mindset wasn't where it is today. I
wasn't envisioning a future filled with children and a shared
home.

We hooked up. The chemistry was off the charts. Alex
seemed to know exactly what I wanted—and he wanted it,
too. At the time, I wasn't dating or looking for love. I was looking for sex, and I had just found really good sex. At the end
of that first evening, Alex walked me to my car, and we had
an awkward (but cute) hug and a kiss goodbye. I remember it
like it was yesterday. We both giggled, smiled, looked into each
other's eyes, and said, "That was an awkward kiss." This seemingly insignificant and silly moment of awkwardness was the
start of something big.

I smiled and left.

It was fun. It was hot. But I had to go "home" and back
into hiding. I had to apply to grad school. I had to escape. Back
to business.

Well, not really. We texted. We had a lot more sex. We went
out on dates. Eventually, I found myself racing to his house.
Speeding down the highway along to Whitney Houston's "So
Emotional." I had the song on repeat. (Unfortunately, that
kind of ruined the song for me.)

I felt alive for the first time ever.

I didn't realize what I had stumbled upon. Alex and I both
seemed to be falling in love with each other.

But Florida was meant to be only a pit stop, not my final
destination. I had gotten into Columbia and the University
of Miami for grad school. Woohoo! But that good news now
became a turning point in my relationship with Alex, like in

the board game Life, where you choose between two paths, each one leading to a completely different future.

I decided to stay in Florida so that Alex and I could be together. And just like that, this one decision would change my life forever. Two months later, Alex and I moved in together. We built a life and a family together. This was something I had never truly experienced, and it felt wonderful. As previously mentioned, I had had relationships before, but this was the first time I was integrating my whole life with someone else's, with the house, the dog, the vacations around the world.

When I met Alex's father, he gave me a big hug and a kiss. It was the first time a father had ever been affectionate with me. Alex and I spent holidays with his family, which were unlike anything I had experienced with mine. His parents and siblings said "I love you" to one another, gave one another presents, hugged, exchanged cards, and celebrated together like something from the Hallmark Channel. It was mind-blowing. I remember the first time I went to one of their gatherings, they got me wonderful gifts—the cologne I had wanted, the running shorts I'd pointed out to Alex, a loving card. I felt uncomfortable because it was all so foreign and unfamiliar, but I loved it nonetheless.

GOOD ENOUGH

In short, I settled. Not for something less, but for a relationship that was good enough.

The concept of a "good enough" relationship was initially introduced to analytical theories by the British psychoanalyst Donald Winnicott. He introduced the idea of the "good enough parent," which suggests that a parent doesn't have to be perfect in order to meet their children's developmental needs. This concept has since been extended to encompass romantic adult partnerships and is a common topic in couples therapy. It emphasizes the importance of accepting that a perfect or ideal partner is not necessary for a fulfilling relationship.

Whenever I advocate on social media to embrace a relationship that is "good enough," I am met with opposition. People assume I mean that they should settle for anything, that they should ignore conflict, even when they're deeply unsatisfied. I do not mean that at all!

What I mean is that a flawless partner or relationship is both unrealistic and impractical. Instead, aim for someone and something that is "good enough." Don't expect that your partner will be a validating machine, and do recognize that problems and disappointments are inevitable in any relationship. What truly matters is that the relationship is predominantly satisfying.

Fortunately, I was able to do this with Alex. I didn't obsess over the potential of finding someone better. I didn't obsess and spiral over whether I wanted to spend the rest of my life with Alex.

I envy that decision now. That twenty-one-year-old me was brave. But it wasn't because I was in a particularly healthy place or meditating daily. It was because I wasn't preoccupied with marriage and children—"the future"—as straight people in my peer group were. I was never pressured to get married; at the time, marriage was not legal for us gays. Also, I was still relatively young then and not even remotely concerned with checking off a list of milestones that now, in my late thirties, feel so incredibly urgent. My experience would probably have been different if I had been straight, raised religiously, or taught from a young age that I should get married by my twenties (as my mother was). This is how our culture, our place in time, and our geography impact how we experience our relationships.

This lack of anxiety allowed me to be fully present with Alex.

Today, I struggle to be present—even while on vacation. There is always something to think about, feel nostalgia for, or obsess over wanting to change. But with Alex, there wasn't. He helped me be present and luxuriate in the moments we shared. The relational hypervigilance I had become accustomed to dissipated when I was with him.

Was that because he was "the One"? No. I don't believe in that.

Was it because I was young and immature? Maybe. But it didn't matter, because I was satisfied and happy. I felt calm and content. Plus, I was having mind-blowing sex daily, which definitely helped the process of settling.

BREAK THE RULES

Or, at the very least, don't let them box you in. Clients and followers on social media frequently ask me about relationship time lines, age gaps, and monogamy versus non-monogamy. These questions often reveal a tension between their personal desires and the societal expectations they've internalized. But: Your life and your relationship belong to you, not to your friends and not to social media influencers. They're yours to shape and enjoy.

Recognizing what we want is an important milestone. The hurdle is often translating this desire into action. That's why we—both you and I—may revert to our culture's rules to assess whether our desires are acceptable, normal, or healthy.

I strongly urge you to reconsider this approach. Don't let others' or society's values dictate your choices. If you feel inclined to move in with your partner immediately, do it! If you want sex right away, go to town! If you'd rather wait for both, that's entirely fine. If you want to take a break from dating altogether, go for it!

I broke them all. To an outsider, Alex and I did it all wrong. We met on an app for casual sex without any intention of dating. We didn't talk about the future or compare our fantasy futures to see if the two were compatible. We were simply focused on being present and having sex.

Because the sex was (very) good, we kept having it. And in doing it, we found our feelings evolving. I fell deeply in love with Alex, and we moved in together four months after that first sexual encounter. Sex continued to be an aspect of our love that felt wonderful to connect over, but it didn't diminish our emotional connection; rather, it only intensified it. If I had been following the presiding rules of our culture—which say that sex isn't a good foundation for a long-term attachment—I never would have met my first love.

Unfortunately, sex is profoundly stigmatized and misconstrued in our culture. The prevailing dating advice suggests that sex is just about lust. We separate sex from love and position it as a distinct entity, sometimes even setting it up as an opposing force to love. We're encouraged not to get confused by lust; we're told that sex isn't love; that people should wait to have sex lest they confuse the two.

The reality is that sex can indeed be an expression of love, a physical manifestation of emotional bonding and intimacy. When shared between two consenting adults in a safe, respectful, and affectionate setting, sex can amplify feelings of love, deepening the connection between partners.

Sex is a love language that conveys feelings that words may fail to capture. In this sense, it's not merely a physical act but a profoundly emotional and psychological experience that can contribute to the quality of a loving relationship.

If you've ever felt a bit out of your depth when it comes to expressing yourself sexually, you're not alone. Let's explore this together.

The Real Story of Sex

Sex begins in the mind and then travels downward.

—MICHAEL BADER

W hen I talk about sex with my clients, they can become noticeably uncomfortable, red in the face, quiet, or squirming in their seats. This reaction, which has been a constant, signals that we're on the right path. That unease is the first step toward embracing comfort and empowerment in one's sexuality.

It begins by acknowledging our collective repressive history, general fears, anxieties, and shame that define sexuality. While many of us have gained more knowledge about sex, just as many continue to grapple with the sex-negative attitudes and values we internalized while growing up. Despite the increase in positive attitudes toward sex, we still find ourselves over-whelmed by a barrage of contradictory messages:

Don't have sex on the first date. Be patient.
Don't wait to have sex.
Have it right away. Find out if you have chemistry.
Sex is important.
Sex isn't important, it's just sex. It's about lust.
Too much sex could mean you're addicted.
A lack of sex means you're not sexually liberated.

We are judged if we do. And we are judged if we don't. These conflicting messages only add to the confusion, shame, and further repression.

It's no surprise that everyone has sexual issues—and I promise you they do. I do, you do, and everyone in your life does. These issues may impact us in different ways and to vary-ing extents, but navigating sexuality within our cultural con-straints is far from a breeze for anyone.

We are about to explore everything about sexuality. As you might already have gleaned, we won't be focusing on the phys-ical aspects, like genitals and orgasms. Instead, we will focus on the cultural contexts in which our sexualities unfold.

As we go through this chapter, I want you to suspend all your preconceived notions about sex. Set aside all the articles, anecdotes, Instagram posts, and other information you've con-sumed on the subject. (No, you cannot simply spice it up by moving your body into a different position. No, you definitely don't need to squirt or shoot buckets of cum or do headstands in order to have a fun and pleasurable sexual experience.) You can let all that go. You never truly needed it, anyway.

Instead, I want you to think about sex in terms of experiences that stimulate and excite your mind and body. It's about your desires. You define your sexuality. It's your body, and no one else should dictate what gives it pleasure. This is how you develop comfort and assertiveness in your sexuality, and that is what I hope to give to you.

REAL SEX

The real story of sex involves a range of intricate relational dynamics and emotional, psychological, and political factors that shape our sexuality. For many people, their sexual narratives remain shrouded in mystery, often neglected, disregarded, and deprioritized.

This brings to mind the case of Jane, a thirty-nine-year-old lesbian cis-female who entered therapy to navigate issues around her sexuality. However, whenever she was asked a question, her face transformed into the hue of a ripe strawberry, cheeks flushed with intense redness. Jane's unease visibly manifested in her physical appearance. I asked her about the discomfort.

"No one has ever asked me such personal questions about my sexuality."

"You've never been asked about your sexuality or your pleasure?"

"No."

"I'm so sorry to hear that, but not surprised. Your sexuality and your pleasure are important!"

Throughout the next year of therapy, I explored with Jane all the nooks and crannies of her sexuality and her erotic life.

While totally common, I am stunned every time; thirty-nine whole years without being asked in-depth questions about one's sexuality? Then again, our parents certainly don't ask us about sex, and few of us have had discussions about sexuality, pleasure, or orgasms in the health-related environments we've occupied.

Sexuality is not something medical doctors receive any training in, and as a result, discussions about sexual health are absent from much of healthcare. Doctors are not instructed to ask questions beyond those related to sexually transmitted infections, sexual behaviors, number of partners—this last is a question they shouldn't be asking; it's irrelevant and is rooted in sex-negative cultural values—and contraceptive use. Inquiries about pleasure, masturbation, and body positivity are usually nonexistent.

Psychotherapists (of all different degrees) also have a lack of such training, and as a result, they often fail to address sexuality in session. Most receive minimal education on the topic, with only one class dedicated to discussing sexuality as a whole (LGBTQ+ issues, penetration, fertility). It's crazy that therapists who work with couples to improve relationship satisfaction don't learn much about one of the most important parts of relationship satisfaction: sex. As a result, almost all my clients enter my office (now a computer screen) having never been asked about sex.

From sex-ed Instagram pages to new sex toy companies—there's more information and permission surrounding sex than ever before. Yet, so many people who struggle with sexual challenges still feel shame about what are, in reality, normal experiences. So, let's start talking about it.

I usually start the conversation with my clients by asking about the last time they had sex or where they first learned about it. One question I ask is "Does orgasm feel good to you?" For a long time, I assumed that orgasms were pleasurable for everyone. But the reality is, not all orgasms are created alike. Sometimes they don't feel as good or make one as euphoric as we assume. This can be for a variety of reasons, from hormonal changes and medications to stress, emotional disconnection, and trauma.

Another question that's interesting to reflect upon is "Where do you masturbate?" One of my clients, Matt, a forty-two-year-old gay cis-male from Turkey, revealed that he masturbated only in the bathroom. He would race to orgasm and then act like it never happened.

"When did you start masturbating?" I asked.

Starting in childhood, Matt hid his masturbation from his parents, for fear of being caught. He was ashamed that he was even masturbating in the first place—so, he rushed the process. The bathroom, a place of hiding, became the one space where he could express his sexuality freely.

Naturally, if you find a certain place comforting, it's up to you whether a change is necessary. Nonetheless, I often encourage my clients to connect with the initial motivations that led them to feel the need to hide, from themselves, when masturbating. And then I push them outside the bathroom.

This is exactly what I did with Matt and other clients (about half of them) who relegate their masturbation to a particular place and into a rushed window of time. I assigned homework: Masturbate in your bed or on the couch, surrounded by cozy pillows. Play some soothing music, light candles, or do whatever you fancy to transform the environment into a warm, inviting space. Select a spot and personalize it. Additionally, I advise them to pace themselves. Relish the process. Pay attention to the escalating pleasure. Remember, reaching orgasm isn't the only objective.

(This is something you should do, too.)

The following week, Matt returned to session proud to report completion of his assignment. He had enjoyed it! "*Sooo* much better than the bathroom," he said. "I didn't even realize what I was doing. It was such a routine. But this one is much better."

Matt no longer masturbates in the bathroom.

I see this with over 50 percent of my cases. Whether it's body shame or leftover shame about their sexuality, many people are masturbating in private areas and rushing without even realizing that more comfortable spaces exist. This transforms masturbation from a task on a to-do list into a soothing escape filled with relaxation and pleasure.

SEX (MIS)EDUCATION

Our early experiences with sex education—or the lack thereof—can shape our lifelong understanding of what is normal or healthy when it comes to sex and relationships. These experiences form the blueprint for how we approach and understand our bodies, self-esteem, and confidence—sexually and nonsexually. When someone receives a thorough, accurate, and sex-positive education, they are more likely to have a healthy, positive attitude toward sex and body esteem.

However, when someone's only exposure to sex is through pornography or movies that portray unrealistic examples of bodies and sexuality (that is, the majority of our population), it's likely they will develop unrealistic expectations about practically everything, from body image to pleasure and orgasm. This often leads to performance anxiety, shame, sexual fear, negative body image, and sometimes even sexual avoidance.

It's a total mindfuck: We expect ourselves and our partners to satisfy us sexually, but we don't learn much (or anything at all) about sex as younger people in order to be able to do that. It's like trying to bake without a recipe.

We are told what to desire. We are told whom to desire. We are told how much is appropriate. We are told how our body should function. But we are never told that sex is for fun, pleasure, and connection, independent of aesthetics or performance.

Again, too many rules.

Culture, social systems, laws, and politics all play a big role in how we understand and think about sex. Sex is not just a biological act but also a historical and cultural process that is shaped by the society we live in. Within this cultural process, everyone will experience sex differently, depending on how safe, comfortable, and uninhibited they feel. This sense of safety is heavily influenced by gender, race, and ethnicity.

In her book *Taking Sexy Back*, Alexandra Solomon writes, "The more marginalized identities you have, the more likely you are to be at war with your body." This highlights how marginalized groups may have a harder time feeling comfortable and safe in their own bodies. Your comfort level with your own sexuality will be impacted, even defined, having been raised in a culture that objectifies people based on their skin color or gender, criminalizes certain sexual orientations, restricts rights to love, or denies access to resources that promote sexual safety and health.

Sexual values and attitudes have changed over time, and they continue to evolve. In the past, premarital sex was shamed and even punished; now it's the norm. An emphasis was historically placed on maintaining the woman's hymen intact, which led to the stigmatization of individuals, particularly women, who had "lost" their virginity. They were often viewed as undesirable or less valuable. We now understand that virginity is a social construct, and we have shifted conversations to focus more on choice, consent, and autonomy.

Masturbation, once frowned upon and discouraged—especially for women—is now understood as a necessary component of sexual health. During the Victorian era, a woman who expressed sexual desire was considered to be suffering from a medical condition and was given the diagnosis of "hysteria." And the treatment . . . the treatment was a "massage" that led to orgasm.

Values around gender and sexual identity have also seen shifts. We have moved beyond the binary of male and female and broadened the spectrum to include a variety of other gender identities. Homosexuality, once thought to be a mental disorder (a literal disease with a diagnosis and a cure), is now accepted as a normal part of human sexuality. Sodomy (anal sex) used to be illegal. Now . . . well, it's not.

Despite this progress, sex remains stigmatized, a taboo subject. Educator and artist Betty Dodson, also known as the original sexual pioneer of the 1960s and '70s, writes, "People who love and explore sex are no different from food connoisseurs, dedicated scientists, or other people who devote time to pursuing a particular interest. When I was an artist working long hours painting, I was admired and rewarded. Once I became interested in spending my time pursuing sex, I was labeled 'nymphomaniac' or, more recently, 'sex addict.'"

While I have not (at least to my knowledge) been labeled a nympho or a sex addict, I am often objectified by people who, because of my work, assume that I'm a sexual machine. This is funny, because my initial interest in sex therapy was largely motivated by my personal struggles with sexuality. It should be noted that the lack of stigma I have received as a sex therapist is likely due to my identity as a gay cis-male. Being both gay and a cis-male, I am *expected* to be hypersexual, whereas by comparison, cis-women are practically viewed as nonsexual beings.

WHY DID YOU BECOME A SEX THERAPIST?

"What's the craziest or kinkiest thing you've ever heard?" I've been asked. "Has a client ever wanted to have sex with you?" Once, I was even asked if I had sex with my clients. This was on a date! Needless to say, we didn't make it to the second one . . .

No, I don't hear "crazy" things. People assume that being a sex therapist is all about dicks, clits, and BDSM dungeon parties, but it's mostly about anxiety and misinformation. Not necessarily the sexy answer people are looking for. While sex therapy certainly involves detailed discussions of sex, it is the relational and psychological processes of how one expresses and experiences their sexuality that are central to the work in session.

So, why did I become a sex therapist? The quick answer? I've had a lot of sexual issues (as most people do) and have worked through them-ish. The long answer? I used to—and sometimes still do—struggle to get aroused and/or to orgasm with new partners. My mind is there—I'm so into it—but my body is simply saying, "Not going to happen." Or, more accurately, "Sorry. I don't feel safe." I learned this early on with Derek.

Derek is a sex therapist. He was influential in my decision to pursue a specialization in sex therapy. He told me stories about his work and shared thoughts about culture and sex. Because I first started seeing him when I was a teenager, I thought that discussions like this were normal in therapy. Derek asked questions about every granular detail of my sexual experience, from arousal and masturbation to partnered sex and eroticism. His questions helped me understand that sex was not a performance, not taboo or shameful, but a pleasurable experience specifically for me to enjoy.

SEX IS NOT A PERFORMANCE

It's common to hear a friend share something about a stressful meeting at work, yet most of our friends aren't talking about how they couldn't get it up the night before. When people experience sexual challenges, they tend to feel broken or ashamed, and in response, they might withdraw from sex. We all grow up learning that our bodies *should* work in a specific way. False!

Thinking about sex as "functional" or "dysfunctional" is unhelpful and harmful. Those labels imply that there is a "normal," or "correct," way to experience sex and that deviations from these norms are unacceptable. This creates feelings of shame or inadequacy for people who don't measure up to these expectations—which most people do not.

This idea of functional versus dysfunctional sex centers on penetration. Historically, sex was defined by penetration because sex was only for procreation. Other forms of sexual expression, such as masturbation and oral or anal sex, were viewed as deviant or abnormal.

I know, ridiculous but true.

While our collective perception of sex has evolved, the focus on penetration still holds strong. Consider the question "When was the last time you had sex?" Chances are, you've just thought about the last time *penetration* was involved. That's because our default idea of sex is closely tied to penetration. For many, sex is synonymous with it. This viewpoint has deep roots in the history of human sexuality.

In short, your sexuality is still organized around an outdated model for sex. It's simply ingrained in our culture's sexual unconscious.

I'm not anti-penetration or anti-orgasm. I am pro-diversity in both sexual expression and experience. After all, when penetration is the only goal, many people are left out.

Sex is a subjective experience and should be defined by an individual's preferences. The real aim of sex is to experience pleasure and fun. And what creates pleasure and fun? Eroticism. Sexual connection, chemistry, and orgasms arise out of the sharing of eroticism, not from specific sexual acts or positions. But don't confuse eroticism with kink or a fetish. Eroticism can be kissing. Or it can be biting, engaging in dirty talk, or exploring a power dynamic.

Unfortunately, many people don't even know what turns them on or off because they haven't been given permission to explore their sexuality freely. The result? Anxiety. There is a shitload of anxiety that manifests in our bodies when we express ourselves sexually.

Performance anxiety affects everyone regardless of age, gender, race, ethnicity, or any other demographic. What's interesting is that we don't consciously register our performance anxiety until after the sex is happening, if at all. But your body is always speaking to you, especially during sex, and it's important to listen up.

HOW PERFORMANCE ANXIETY WORKS

Our bodies complete a variety of complex tasks that happen below our conscious level of awareness. Sex is no different. During any kind of sexual activity, whether partnered or solo, our bodies cook up a storm to create the sexual responses of arousal, pleasure, and orgasm. This involves the release of hormones and neurotransmitters such as serotonin, norepinephrine and epinephrine, dopamine, oxytocin, and prolactin. Without these chemicals, our sexual responses would slow or stop completely. This, in turn, would lead to a decline in arousal, pleasure, and definitely orgasm.

If something feels even slightly off, the body will consciously or unconsciously slow the release of these important sex hormones. Why? Because our body prioritizes threat over pleasure. But threat doesn't necessarily include physical danger. It could be anything ranging from perceived rejection to the anticipation of physical pain. So, if during sex you think even for a millisecond, "Oh no, what if they don't like what I am doing?" or "Oh, this might hurt or be uncomfortable," your body will slowly start to sound the alarm. Keep in mind this also includes a variety of unconscious influences about your level of emotional safety and trust. You don't have to be thinking about fear in order to be afraid. When this happens, your body releases the stress hormones adrenaline and cortisol, which produce higher levels of anxiety. (Goodbye arousal!) And at this point, pleasure fades. This is how the psychological can impact the biological, and then the biological in turn can impact the psychological, both consciously and unconsciously.

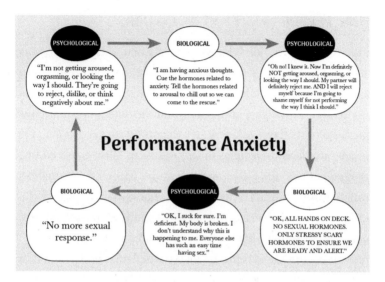

We all operate with a performance-based model for sex because this is how sex is understood in the culture to which we belong. This is the model in place when we first learned about sex, and unless we consciously decide to use a different one, it will remain our model. If you do decide to learn a new way to experience your sexuality (you're doing it right now), know that it will take practice. Because sex is a skill. Sometimes it takes many years of practice to hone your sexual skills and create change. I've been doing it for decades, and I still experience challenges.

Why? Because sex is psychological. Have you ever felt physically aroused, but the pleasure was dull or you weren't feeling "into" it? That's because you weren't psychologically aroused.

Psychological arousal is heavily shaped by emotional and relational dynamics.

Your experience of psychological arousal is dependent on your personal sexual and nonsexual histories. There's a helpful model for this: the Dual Control Model of Sexual Response, identified by Drs. John Bancroft and Erick Janssen in the late 1990s. This model gives us an automobile metaphor that is broken down into two different systems: the accelerator (the gas) and the brakes. The sexual accelerator and the sexual brakes are two separate parts that work together to control sexual arousal. The accelerator leads to feelings of arousal, as in "I'm so turned on." Simultaneously, the brake system can be triggered by anything, ranging from distraction to turnoffs. These systems manifest in unique ways. One person might have a strong accelerator system, which leads to high levels of sexual desire, while another might have an incredibly sensitive brake system. And others might have both.

Emily Nagoski's book *Come as You Are* sheds light on the issue of desire and its context (yes, that word again). As Nagoski points out, "The problem isn't the desire itself, it's the context." We first have to become aware of our accelerator and brakes and then consciously make an effort to activate the accelerator and reduce the factors that slam on the brakes. Think about the relational dynamic with your partner: how safe you feel, how you feel about your body. Even the temperature of the room or the aroma of something that has nothing to do with sex could impact your psychological brakes.

I have a very sensitive brake system, and even small distractions make me less interested. Someone could say the wrong word or make a silly noise, and I'd be immediately turned off.

And aromas? Forget about it! I am the *most* reactive to odors. However, this sensitivity was reduced and almost disappeared entirely once I got into my relationship with Alex.

Alex and I had a wonderful sexual connection, and our chemistry felt exhilarating. It was in this relationship that I felt liberated to explore kink and eroticism in ways I never had before. I would learn just how comfortable I could feel naked and noisy (farty) in my imperfect body. I felt attended to both sexually and, more important, emotionally. It was in that comfort that my lifelong anxiety and depression dissipated. The safety I felt in my relationship allowed for it.

When the relationship ended, I assumed that I would continue feeling sexually liberated. But the exact opposite happened. My butt clenched (literally, with fear). Sexually, I regressed. I hadn't been with anyone else for ten years minus the few threesomes Alex and I had had. Having sex with strangers was difficult for me. I wanted to be there (like, really wanted it), but my body wasn't cooperating. There was a huge difference between how I expressed myself sexually in the context of my long-term relationship and how I expressed myself amid the unknown contexts with short-term or casual sex partners. With Alex, I knew him and, therefore, felt comfortable and safe expressing myself. With casual sex partners, however, I knew little of how they felt about me or if they would be sticking around. Consciously, I felt safe, but unconsciously, my body was telling a different story. I often retreated into myself.

Casual sex is hot in theory, but my experiences of it in the moment were mostly hit or miss. There is a great deal of pressure, especially for gay cisgender men, to seek out and enjoy casual sex like necessary nutrition. As a sex therapist, I greatly valued sex and wanted to have it, but I also knew myself. At times, it felt like just too much of a gamble when I could simply go home and masturbate. And at other times, I'd crave the touch of someone else and try again.

Anxiety can serve as an invisible force guiding our sexual interactions, regardless of whether we consciously acknowledge it. Our behaviors and actions can reveal the hidden anxiety within us. When we prioritize our partner's pleasure over our own during a sexual encounter, retreating into ourselves, this is usually an indication of underlying anxiety and even of an unconscious expression of sexual shame or disconnection.

I want you to stop having sex the way you think your *partner* wants to have sex and start having sex the way *you* want to have sex. It's your body. It's your sexuality. If you want to experience arousal and pleasure, you must first connect and cater to your body, not someone else's. Focusing on your own pleasure doesn't mean your partner's pleasure doesn't matter. In fact, we can connect better with others sexually when we are better connected to ourselves. This also goes for all other, nonsexual relational dynamics, which we will get into later.

Think about this: Would you go to dinner and order for yourself only what your partner ordered? If you did, would you enjoy it? You might enjoy eating what they chose, but you would definitely enjoy eating something you chose. And it's tough to feel satisfied if you're not eating what you crave.

At the end of the day, you need to find out what works for you (not someone else). If you don't want penetration, that's wonderful. If you do—great! If you don't like casual sex and want to wait, that's great. If you want to have sex with a stranger on the street, that's great, too. It doesn't matter. What matters is that you feel safe and comfortable and that you are able to get aroused enough to experience pleasure. Any perceived value or social pressure that is incongruent with your own desires and preferences simply does not apply to you. Stop trying to fit your sexuality into the limiting box you were handed by your culture. Your sexual expression is a highly subjective experience specific to you.

If you want to grow sexually, you must let go of the expectation that your body should work in one culturally determined way. Sex is not just about genitals banging together. It's about *much much more. Sex is relational.* It's never *just* sex.

Sex is full of meaning—if you're willing to look for it. You can learn a lot about someone from how they express themselves or avoid themselves sexually, whether that involves eroticism and fantasy or their inability to answer when asked, "So, what do you like?" This is what psychotherapist Esther Perel meant with her famous question "Tell me how you were loved, and I will tell you how you make love." Sex has just as much meaning as love does. However, how we give and receive love gets more attention than how we engage in erotic touch.

Sex requires relational skills, and learning these skills will have a ripple effect across all areas of your life.

Good Sex Requires:
- Communication;
- Boundaries;
- Body comfort and esteem;
- Self-awareness;
- Self-esteem and confidence; and
- Selfishness and self-care.

What gets in the way of developing these skills is—you guessed it—anxiety and unresolved trauma. But often, people have so many barriers up that they can't even broach the topic.

THOMAS: "I CAN'T TALK ABOUT SEX"

My client Thomas, a thirty-eight-year-old white heterosexual cisgender male, came to therapy while he was single. Shortly thereafter, he met someone special. (I get so excited when my clients discover love, as it gives me hope, and it's interesting to see how transformative the power of a deep connection can be.) I asked Thomas about the sex.

They hadn't had any.

I asked about sexual discussions.

They hadn't had any.

I said, "This is good news! You have a lot to talk about and explore. How exciting!" And it truly is. Because most clients are freaked out about having sex with someone new, I try to model some level of excitement for them. After all, it's sex, not a punishment (unless that's what you're into).

Over several sessions, I encouraged Thomas to initiate conversations about sex with his partner. Despite being a highly sexual person, he found it difficult and would often say things like "I just couldn't." As months went by, the two had a drunken hookup one night, but their sexual connection otherwise remained an unexplored mystery. Neither of them had taken the initiative, and they never discussed it. For this reason, we shifted in session to understanding the underlying reasons behind Thomas's resistance. It should be noted that when confronting sexual challenges many people are too quick to only focus on the superficial layers of the here-and-now issue.

While at times helpful, there is usually much more unfolding that you don't want to miss.

It turned out that Thomas was stuck, not because he was disconnected from his desires or was experiencing performance anxiety but rather because he had a history of anxiety and relational trauma within his family of origin. (Most sexual issues can be traced to some form of a relational trauma.) While growing up, he wasn't allowed to be himself. His parents neither asked nor cared what he wanted; they both worked late hours and modeled avoidance and emotional disconnection. Thomas denied having been harmed by his parents' style of caregiving, but unresolved feelings of withdrawal and avoidance of vulnerable interactions were manifesting in his adult life, particularly in his inability to connect sexually with his new partner.

Talking about sex, let alone having it, demands a deep level of self-disclosure and vulnerability. But Thomas was never allowed to be open as a child; instead, he learned to hide his true self, his thoughts, emotions, and desires. Just as his parents, we learned in session, had hid theirs. As a result, when it came to anything sexual, Thomas lost himself to the point where he couldn't speak. This was the silence and withdrawal of his childhood.

Thomas isn't the only one whose early experiences of being silenced (nonsexually) were expressed during sex.

CLAUDIA: ORGASM CHECKLIST

Claudia struggled with something similar. A twenty-eight-year-old white heterosexual cisgender female who wanted to date, she felt stuck and lonely. She'd grown up in a religious community that condemned everything related to sex, especially in women. And as therapy progressed, it became clear that Claudia was still struggling with the shame she had learned in early childhood. As we worked through this, her overall feeling of shame decreased and her confidence increased.

However, she still struggled to orgasm during partnered sex. Claudia explained that her preferred method of masturbation made it impossible to replicate the same feelings during penetrative sex. When masturbating alone, Claudia had to be on her back and would use a vibrator. She felt so anxious about introducing a vibrator into partnered sex that she took orgasms off the table for herself.

I hear this *all* the time. It's not a gender-specific problem. Everyone has a very specific way they orgasm. Sometimes people have multiple roads toward increasing their pleasure and eventually an orgasm. Other times, not so much. Many people actually have a checklist in order to reach orgasm. This was the case for Claudia and me. This isn't a bad thing. If you want to orgasm, the important part is knowing how to get there.

When this kind of thing happens, I say, "This is great news. Just do with your partner whatever you do during masturbation!"

Claudia quietly responded, "I don't feel comfortable, though. I'm afraid he'll judge me, and he always says he wants to get me off."

I immediately bounced back with "Do you think it could be possible that your partner would take pleasure in your experiencing pleasure?"

The idea of receiving pleasure without having to take care of her partner (something she had never been able to do within her family) stirred up the shame Claudia had learned throughout childhood and adolescence. Shame caused her to deprioritize her own pleasure just as her parents had taught her and just as the larger society had taught her to do as a woman. She withdrew and retreated. Some would say that withdrawing when engagement is required is an unconscious expression of shame or anxiety. In Claudia's case, it was both.

Together we peeled back the layers of Claudia's pleasure. On the one hand, a simple logistical shift would allow her to experience deep pleasure. But her earlier narratives of shame and anxiety were triggered (just as they were with Thomas) and prevented her from being able to make those logistical changes. Over time, in therapy, I was able to convince Claudia to experiment. And I'm happy to report that she learned how to get what she needed out of partnered sex. Her vibrator is now always a fixture of her night table.

Honestly, I can't recall a single instance where the major barrier to someone expressing their sexuality wasn't shame, anxiety, and a lack of communication.

JAMES: PENETRATION PRESSURE

Meet James, a thirty-year-old heterosexual cis-male whom I had been seeing for several years. James's primary issue was around penetration—specifically, his struggle to orgasm through it. The logical solution would be to shift focus from penetration and toward something more pleasurable. However, James was resistant to doing so. Why? Because he had learned the rule that penis owners should maintain an erection and be able to orgasm through penetration, and he harbored the assumption that his partner would be disappointed if he couldn't meet that expectation.

Getting James to communicate his struggles took some

persuasion, but eventually he did open up to his partner, who reacted positively. The conversation centered on sexual preferences, but for James, revealing these preferences felt akin to disclosing a deeply held secret. Following the discussion, he experienced a boost in confidence, and his partner became more open about their own desires. Ultimately, this communication enriched many aspects of the couple's life.

Without a doubt, there's a dance of complexity when it comes to sex. It's not simply a physical act—there's always a more profound, captivating mystery to unravel.

SEXUALITY IS POWER, CONFIDENCE, AND FREEDOM

Sex is more than just a physical act. Its physicality intertwines with the psychological and emotional, with self-esteem; with fear of rejection, of unworthiness; and even with aspects of depression. However, it also has the potential to serve as a transformative space, fostering self-esteem, addressing and alleviating fears of rejection, cultivating a sense of worthiness, and contributing to overall contentment and happiness. Therapist Ian Kerner says, "Desire is more than what happens between the sheets. It's about how you live your life."

Across all my cases, as I have helped people increase their sexual confidence, I have consistently observed positive transformations in their lives—in their self-esteem, their relational satisfaction, their body image.

One of the most challenging barriers for folks is prioritizing their own pleasure. That means not just having sex the way their partner wants and not withholding their own desires. This requires a level of selfishness that, historically, during childhood, was never allowed or encouraged.

When we focus on our own pleasure, we are required to let go of concerns for the other person's pleasure for a moment. In his book *Arousal: The Secret Logic of Sexual Fantasies,* Dr. Michael J. Bader writes, "Sexual excitement requires that we momentarily become selfish and turn away from concerns about the other's pleasure in order to surrender to our own, that we momentarily stop worrying about hurting or rejecting the other person. We need to have the capacity to 'use' another person without concerns that the other will feel used."

Of course, Bader is not talking about a nonconsensual "using" of others; that would be harmful. I imagine even reading the word *use* might be triggering for some readers. Keep in mind that the using Bader is talking about is not at the expense of someone else's safety, pleasure, or connection. It's in service to our own, which is also in service to our partner's, as being present with ourselves creates an exciting, vulnerable dynamic that's necessary for sexual connection. With this "using," there is no disregarding of the other person, but rather a relinquishing of the desire to take care of our partner in moments when we feel powerful enough to access arousal and, therefore, increase our own pleasure. It is a letting go of the fear, shame, guilt, responsibility, and burden inherent in limiting relational dynamics that allows for this process to unfold.

It's like eating a meal with your partner. If you're not enjoying the dish you've both ordered, would you continue eating it just because your partner is? Of course not. You would adjust the seasoning, or even order takeout later if you found your dish inedible. Similarly, during sex, it's important to focus on your own arousal and pleasure. This doesn't mean you don't care about your partner, but it does mean you shouldn't continue sex if it isn't wonderfully delicious and pleasurable for you, too. Just as you wouldn't force yourself to eat something you didn't like, you shouldn't force yourself to engage in any sexual experience that doesn't bring you pleasure and joy.

Of course, eating is not as vulnerable an act as sex is. That is why I see sex as the final frontier of adulthood, a place where vulnerability and intimacy are intertwined. But it's also a place where our deepest fears and insecurities can arise, fueled by the shame and guilt of our past.

It's precisely in these moments of vulnerability that we have the opportunity to confront and overcome our childhood anxieties and relational fears. It's then that we are given the chance to reclaim our power and rewrite our narrative.

The Honeymoon Is Over

Love isn't something natural. Rather it requires discipline, concentration, patience, faith, and the overcoming of narcissism. It isn't a feeling, it is a practice.

—ERICH FROMM

I see most couples in therapy years, even decades, after the resentment, hatred, and hopelessness in their relationships have become a monstrous mountain that is terrifying, even to me. And yes, I tell my clients this, especially when one or both of them seem unbothered (numb and disconnected) by that mountain, which is often.

They come in armed with laundry lists of unfulfilled needs, criticisms, and expectations that look more like science fiction than any kind of real human relationship.

They're not like me.

They don't see me.

We want different things.

They don't share their emotions.

She's critical.

He's unemotional.

They're always in a bad mood.

Change them.

I shouldn't have to put up with this.

By this point, both partners feel an incredible amount of pressure to make the relationship work or to end it. The result is a polarizing hostage situation where one or both people hold their partner in contempt, demanding that they change, or else!

TERRI AND PETER: CHILDHOOD RE-ENACTMENTS

Terri, a forty-two-year-old cisgender Hispanic woman who identifies as bisexual, and Peter, a thirty-year-old Polish American white heterosexual cis-male, had been a couple for five years and moved in together during Covid-19. Upon entering therapy, it was clear that the two had a deep connection to each other, but they were hyper-focused on resolving conflict.

In the beginning of their relationship, when they lived apart, they felt free, and their dynamic was easygoing, with little to no conflict. But once they decided to move in together, and their intimacy grew, conflicts began to arise.

INTIMACY OVER TIME

When people talk about growing "intimate," they usually mean having sex or enjoying some vague idea of emotional closeness. When I use the word *intimacy*, particularly when referring to a couple, I'm referring to a deepening understanding of another person based on ongoing experiences with them over an extended period and across a variety of contexts. With many couples (for instance, Terri and Peter), moving in together increases intimacy. You see all your partner's moods, quirks, and habits along a spectrum from the good and bad to the ugly.

During any external shift—such as moving in together—couples can experience a marked change in the dynamic of their relationship. Any significant change to the fundamental structure of a relationship, such as moving in together, having children, or job loss, can impact everything from the flow of sexual desire to how we perceive our partner. Such a shift happened with Terri and Peter: After they moved in together, their honeymoon phase came to a screeching halt.

Despite my efforts to encourage self-reflection, Terri and Peter appeared resistant to exploring their personal histories; each was convinced they were not to blame. Terri expressed apprehension over the future of their relationship, citing Peter's perceived immaturity and inability to meet her needs. These concerns heightened the anxiety about her age and ability to have children, leading her to reassess their relationship.

Meanwhile, Peter appeared stressed and bewildered; he felt he was making every effort to address Terri's concerns while still being unable to alleviate her distress.

Each was scared of losing the other, but the more they tried to hold on to their relationship, the more they pushed each other away. This happens a lot with couples. They want so badly to fix things, to grow closer as a couple, that the way they go about it often only pushes them further apart. You will see this in all the cases I describe throughout this book.

In therapy, Terri and Peter finally began to explore their respective histories and behavioral patterns in order to understand why each would react or act toward the other in ways that led to disconnection. Both had grown up in families where conflict was constant, and both had often found themselves at the center of that conflict. However, their reactions to their respective families' disagreements were quite different. Terri would retaliate by confronting and fighting back, whereas Peter would retreat and shut down. While these responses might have been adaptive and necessary during childhood, they no longer served them as adults in their relationship.

A typical session with Terri and Peter would go something like this:

TERRI: Every time we have a conflict, you fight me on it. Can't you just listen and validate me? I'm constantly thinking about having kids, and then these conflicts come up and I'm like—do I even want to raise a child in this space? Do *I* even want to be in this space? It makes me feel unsafe and unprotected when you do this. Like you'll never understand me.

PETER: I just . . . You're right. I don't understand you,

Terri. I feel like I'm trying everything I can to make this work. Sometimes when we have a conflict, you deny *my* feelings, so I am in some ways defending myself and/or re-explaining my side of the story. What else am I supposed to do? I am trying. But it feels like it's never enough. I'll just be quiet and not say anything because . . .

ME: Okay, pause. [The amount of interrupting I do in session is wild and kind of exhilarating.] Let me just lay out some themes here. Terri, things I'm hearing from you: *invalidated, misunderstood, unsafe, powerless.* Would you agree?

TERRI: Yes. Except the *powerless* one. I don't feel powerless. I feel empowered when I speak my mind.

ME: You might feel empowered when you speak your mind (which is great), but when you hold Peter fully responsible for your relational future, you render yourself . . . well, powerless.

TERRI: Ohhh. Okay. Right.

ME: Okay, and Peter, the themes I'm getting from you are: You're feeling invisible, misunderstood, powerless, hope-less, and collapsed—meaning just totally shut down.

PETER: Yes.

ME: Do any of these themes sound familiar to either of you?

TERRI: Yes. Growing up.

ME: *Yessss!* Your childhood. And the two of you are re-sponding in the same ways you did as kids. Terri, I un-derstand you were often the target of conflict growing up, and you learned to engage directly; you fought for your space because no one gave it to you without its involving major criticism or abandonment. And Peter, you learned to withdraw and become small because your mother and sister constantly criticized and berated you. After a while, you stopped trying. This is what the both of you are doing with each other. *And and and*—you're using the words on each other that really should be directed at your parents. Because, as I see it, both of you are sitting in a therapy room desperately trying to make things work. Which is not something either of your families did for you. That's a big deal. That's powerful. That's differentiation.

PETER: Yeah, I guess when things get tough, I do tend to feel undervalued. So, after a small fight, I just shut down. It's how I coped back then.

TERRI: And I feel like I need to stand up for myself, just like I did when I was a kid. Like, I shouldn't tolerate some of these things. If I'm feeling a certain way, and Peter just focuses on damage control, it feels invalidating, like what I grew up with.

ME: Good. Recognizing these patterns is the first step. Now let's explore what healthy conflict can look like for both of you. It's important to understand that conflict is inevitable and that it can be an opportunity for growth and deeper connection. And not only that, but unlike in your family, you can both have an impact on the relationship!

Their first challenge was to end the cycle of responding from a childlike place. Their second challenge was to normalize conflict and explore what healthy conflict could look like. Healthy conflict for Terri and Peter looked like communicating with the understanding that they were both there for each other. This helped them rebrand the earlier model of conflict (scary, threatening, and lonely) from their childhoods to something that was . . . yes, still frustrating and annoying, but more collaborative, understanding, and safe. This also helped them accept the inevitability of conflict and use it as an opportunity for connection. By letting go of their fear of conflict and the need to control each other, and by being more vulnerable, they were able to build a stronger, more authentic connection.

The end of the "honeymoon period" is an important part of a relationship. All couples, like Terri and Peter, will inevitably reach this crossroads in their relationship. However, when conflicts arise, few take the necessary step of seeking professional help and, instead, resort to arguing or withdrawing from each other, which can ultimately end the relationship.

Here is the hard truth: The honeymoon phase has an expiration date. No matter how blissful it feels in the beginning, the idealization will eventually fade and often transform into disillusionment. Therefore, it's crucial to stabilize any impulsive reactions to this common relational phase. No red flag need be waved or alarm bell rung. Rather, consider the end of the honeymoon phase as your chance to develop deeper intimacy with your partner.

This is partly what happened to me.

ALEX AND ME

Alex and I? We were different: I wanted to work out. He wanted to watch TV. I wanted to stay in. He wanted to go out. He wanted to party late. I wanted to be in bed by ten (at the latest; now it's even earlier). I tried to eat as mindfully as possible. He loved Wendy's. When we traveled, he wanted to go to gay dive bars, and I wanted to go to cocktail lounges. He expressed anger, and I shut down in silence. He didn't communicate his emotions. I did. I wanted to have deep conversations. He did not.

Despite these differences big and small, our relationship was the only thing that had ever brought me happiness. Up until I met Alex, I had been a depressed, anxious, cynical nihilist.

I've always journaled, typing on my computer. My journal was the place where I would talk about how miserable I was. Every sad, disturbing, random thought goes into that document. But for the first three years of my relationship with Alex, I didn't write anything. And when I revisited the journal, what I found there slapped me in the face.

"It's been a while. I haven't written b[e]c[ause] I haven't had the need . . . I've been happy."

Mic drop. *What?* Me, happy for an extended period? S'cuse me? I was a professional anxious depressive, so this was truly wild news to read.

When you've been through trauma or have had ongoing mental health problems, the experience often feels terminal. I had clung to that narrative. I had identified with my wounds. It was all I knew, the only thing that made sense to me.

At least until I met Alex.

He and I got along well because we had a lot of fun together and because our sexual chemistry was on fire. We talked to each other in baby voices and gave each other cute little nicknames. And somehow, Alex was able to have a sweet surprise for me every day. Some days, it was my favorite meal (salmon with Béarnaise sauce and asparagus). Other days, it would be a random object he had found at a store that he thought would make our life easier. Little things I couldn't have thought of on my own.

The beginning of our relationship was uncomplicated. We lived together; we both worked jobs with predictable schedules, doing work we didn't bring home with us. We moved into a beautiful oceanfront condo. Imagine having sex on the twenty-sixth floor, with all the windows open and the sound of ocean waves wafting in from outside. It was heaven. Alex was satisfied at work, and I was calm knowing I had grad school coming up and the next few years mapped out. We had wonderful adventures, traveling all over the world. Life was good.

Yes, we had a few bumps in the road, but the relationship was relatively easy, with low conflict. If we had a little squabble now and then, we'd repair it through humor (baby voices), sex, and food. It was three years into our relationship, and I was twenty-four at the time. I wasn't thinking about children, marriage, or any other major relationship milestone or commitment, so the pressure on our relationship to be moving in any direction, other than decorating our condo, was nonexistent.

LET'S TALK ABOUT THAT PRESSURE

The pressure to meet relational milestones can be disruptive. It is a huge barrier to connection and will often stop any relationship from developing if one or both gets a whiff of incompatibility. Why? Because people are so focused on trying to control a future that hasn't even happened yet.

Shockingly, I didn't have this problem when I was young. Now when I go on a first date and start fantasizing right away about having a relationship with them and where it could lead, I think, *Will they want to be bicoastal with me? Do they want kids? Would they be a good co-parent?* It's out of control—but, again, something so many of us struggle with.

It's not that you shouldn't fantasize about a future or reflect upon these questions. But attempting to anticipate a future with someone who is a literal stranger is for sure a case of self-protection—which is also okay. But as we've learned, self-protection can get in the way of our actually being present enough to see whom we have in front of us.

So, dream, fantasize—but limit your time doing so. And if a concern about your partner comes up, ask them! Otherwise, be present and see if you can relax into the moment and connect. At least, this is what I tell myself. (It's often easier said than done.)

Alex was the first partner I had ever lived with, so my focus was primarily on that first positive experience of "home." We decorated, created our own traditions around holidays, went shopping for vintage furniture on weekends, and even started refinishing some pieces we found. This type of connection wasn't something I had ever experienced.

Then, graduate school started, and I began to change. And these changes impacted the way I saw Alex and experienced our relationship.

No relationship can be without challenge or conflict for too long. (Although, mind you, we did make it four-plus years until . . . Cue the end of the honeymoon phase! Enter the disappointment and disillusionment phase!) And as I mentioned earlier, the end of the honeymoon phase is a defining feature in the evolution of any relationship. We could even say it is the *real* start of the relationship. It's the moment when the ideals we envisioned for the relationship come crashing down and we finally realize we haven't chosen our knight in shining armor after all. Disappointed, we now find our partner imperfect and, at times, infuriating.

This is one of the hardest parts of a relationship. So, I will let you down gently: Anyone you love will disappoint you. They will be a mixture of all the wonderful things you thought they were and all the absolutely frustrating things you thought you wouldn't ever again have to deal with in a partner. I'm sorry to break it to you, but if you want to move toward a more mature version of love, you will have to let go of idealized futures and other fantasies and accept the brutal reality that your partner, like all human beings, will be fundamentally flawed. (News flash: You are, too; it goes both ways.)

I saw only later that Alex and I were at an important crossroads. This was an opportunity for us to revisit the unspoken contract of our commitment and co-author a second edition. But . . . we didn't. We had never established any ground rules for having hard conversations about triggers, disappointments, needs, fulfillment, or boundaries. Relationship and love advice wasn't plastered all over the internet and social media. No one was talking about relationships as we do today. Back then, neither of us even registered that this could be an important thing to do.

On the one hand, our ability to either avoid or tolerate conflict created the illusion of stability. Yet, on the other hand, this mutual avoidance left our partnership vulnerable to unresolved and unsolvable conflict. Neither of us had ever learned the words or acquired the skills necessary to talk about the things that threatened our relationship. This led to distance and a lack of connection, and our challenges grew only larger . . . and into one of those scary mountains I see in my clients. In short, Alex and I co-created an avoidant dynamic that was familiar to both of us.

This is something I regret, and something I would encourage you to investigate ASAP if you're in a relationship. If you haven't already, start now. Consider crafting a relationship contract that lays out the foundations and guidelines for the various facets of your relationship, including the inevitable conflicts that arise. While the content of the contract is up to you, I recommend that it address how you'll handle a range of issues such as disappointments, conflicts, differences in needs and desires, frustrations, communication styles, and mismatched libidos. Essentially, address all potential challenges proactively, in the abstract, before they become concrete, real-world problems. Also, begin having these conversations from the start of your relationship, so that when challenges inevitably arise in years two, five, ten, or twenty, you will already have the language and tools required to navigate them. Many couples are not proactive in their communication because they never learned how to be, but it's never too late to start.

DO AS I SAY, NOT AS I DID . . .

But I didn't bring it up. And *Alex* certainly didn't bring it up. We didn't talk about any of it, and it became a problem. Because life got in the way, as it always does.

Changes to the external environment can lead to internal changes that can, in turn, change our relationships. My entering graduate school brought about a profound shift. As my world began to broaden, and as I started to engage with diverse perspectives, I noticed a parallel shift in my understanding of my bond with Alex. This academic transition wasn't merely a change in my educational status, but it was an evolution in my mental, emotional, and intellectual landscape. I was using a new lens through which to scrutinize life and, by extension, my relationship with Alex. For better or worse.

I started to understand the importance of open communication, emotional intelligence, and mutual growth in a relationship. The more I immersed myself in my studies, the more I began to question the dynamics of our relationship. It wasn't about Alex or me individually; it was about how we, as a unit, failed to adapt to our evolving understandings. We hadn't anticipated these challenges and, thus, were unequipped to deal with the subsequent emotional turmoil.

When I finished grad school and started working in my practice, uncertainty loomed. I had to think about the future, and I started to obsess over everything. I was preoccupied with analyzing every detail of my family and my life in general. I had begun a new chapter for myself, but Alex was still enjoying the satisfaction of his present chapter. He had moved to Florida from New York City a few years before I did and had worked hard to get where he was when we met. He was seven years older than me, so we were at completely different developmental milestones. He was settling into work, and I was just starting to figure it all out.

As time went on, more differences began to develop or became more evident. And they weren't logistical or developmental;

they were emotional. While these differences were present be-fore, they grew into something more concerning—to me, at least.

We had completely different emotional styles. At the beginning of our relationship, I wasn't fully aware of what an emotional style even was, let alone how to navigate my own. At twenty-one, I had yet to fully separate myself from my family. Our four-plus years of living together in Florida, plus learn-ing about relationships, love, and family systems in graduate school, had accelerated my self-exploration. Basically, I had found my voice, at least internally.

Being able to use it with Alex was another story.

I had been in therapy since I was a kid, and not only had Alex never been, but he didn't value self-reflection. I was deeply invested in self-help and personal growth, and he had read one self-help book about being gay and was completely disinter-ested in any other self-reflective/growth-oriented activity.

Alex wasn't unemotional; he was actually very emotionally expressive, but he lacked the curiosity needed to delve deeper into the cause of his emotions. He also appeared to be unin-terested in or unaware of how to inquire about my emotional state. As a result, he didn't communicate or express empathy in the same ways I did. As a deep thinker (an overanalyzer at times), I felt alone and hopeless. The situation also made me feel as if I weren't allowed to be different or to use my new voice.

And yet . . . On the other hand, this person, who wouldn't always ask how my day was . . .

Loved me dearly. He kissed and cuddled me. He held me when I cried about my family (sadly, a regular occurrence).

He fucked me regularly and prioritized my pleasure. He had dinner waiting for me when I came home. (He had gone to culinary school and was a talented chef.) He was lighthearted and only wanted to have fun. With me.

Being loved by Alex felt good. The relationship I had with him was the best I had ever had, including but not limited to connections with past intimate partners, family members, and friends. Being with someone who cared about me was huge. The feeling of home and safety we had together was something I had never experienced, and it was just what I needed. Alex's caring and loving approach helped me feel less sad about losing family members over and over again. Despite our differences, the relationship was good enough, and this level of satisfaction de-emphasized the threat our differences actually posed.

As I dealt with our differences internally, other, external problems started to emerge that had to do with how our relationship was set up: We were codependent. Alex was my best friend, social network partner, life companion, lover, roommate, family, and travel buddy. But, again, I wanted to have deeper conversations, and Alex wasn't interested. Without any friends, I felt isolated, unable to be what, at the time, I thought was my authentic self.

When I first moved to Florida, I struggled to make friends. I didn't think I would be staying, so I never put myself out there or took any social risks. Then Alex came along, and I stayed for him, putting all my effort and time into the relationship, building our home and family together—one of the most rewarding experiences of my life. But the consequence was that I never made any friends of my own—not even in grad school. Alex was my everything. And while this was cute in some ways, it became a problem after seven years.

I now know that my having friends besides Alex would have taken the pressure off our relationship, off Alex, to satisfy me intellectually. Most couples have trouble with this. Finding a balance between independence and dependence is an ongoing challenge.

But there's no need to freak out about such missteps. (Just don't ignore them.) Whether your relationship has become codependent, you've lost parts of yourself, or you've failed to address important conflicts, it's okay. We could even say that such challenges are normal, unavoidable, and important for growth. While they may appear to be threats, they are also opportunities to reevaluate and connect. You may want guidelines for optimal balance, a solution for how to manage this persistent challenge, but there aren't any. It's up to you and your partner.

Here's the one thing I can tell you: Be sure to create a social life outside your relationship. This isn't just about having friends. It's about differentiation, an important concept I will be discussing often. (Keep it in mind as you read on.) Differentiation is about learning how to be independent while remaining positively connected to your partner. That means establishing a certain level of separateness so the relationship doesn't buckle under the weight of total dependence.

Without independence and autonomy, my total reliance on Alex for all my needs only magnified the missing pieces, posing a threat to the warm, loving sense of home I had grown to appreciate.

What I loved about Alex was his lightness, his silliness and creativity. These were, after all, what had initially drawn me to him. As the relationship continued and our intimacy grew, it became harder for me to stay connected to these qualities because I felt so lost about who I was, who Alex was, and what that meant for my life.

It was as if, unconsciously, I wanted Alex to give me permission to self-express. I wanted Alex to rescue me. I wasn't taking responsibility for what I should have been giving to myself. In the here and now, all my complaints felt explicitly related to him. At the time, I kept wishing he were different, that it was his fault.

I started with the "if onlys":

If only he became self-aware.
If only he *wanted* to become self-aware.
If only he learned to communicate his emotions.
If only he came to bed with me, an hour earlier.
If only we did a yoga class together.

I was trying to change him. And if you're at this place in your relationship, it's time for a big pause.

It's important to honor and respect our partners' differences, limitations, and perceived flaws while maintaining a positive connection to the parts of them you love. And if you can't, it's something you should negotiate as soon as possible. You might be convinced that it is your partner who needs to change, but it's actually both of you. Otherwise, your intolerance can lead you to feel contempt. And intolerance and contempt are relationship killers.

It's not just me. We all want to try to change our partner at times to better suit our needs. To minimize having to negotiate differences. But relationships don't work like that. Each person has their own set of beliefs, values, and characteristics that can't simply be changed. And if you do try to change or blame in the form of being convinced that they need to change, this will create resentment and conflict and will undermine the mutual respect and acceptance upon which healthy relationships are built.

I also felt entitled to Alex's interior world; I wanted to know everything. But it wasn't that Alex wouldn't share that world with me; it's that he couldn't. He just wasn't curious enough to reflect on his inner life in the same way I did. I wanted him to interview me, to ask all the questions, but again, that's simply not how Alex experienced the world, thought, or communicated. And while I told myself this was because he didn't care, it was actually quite the opposite.

I didn't know what I wanted, but my entire being had been drawn to Alex. Unconsciously, it was clear: I was being drawn to everything that I was missing from childhood. My family was emotionally absent, and it was threatening. Alex brought fun, laughter, and lots of pleasure. Indeed, it was this lightness that had drawn me into the relationship with him in the first place. Yet, now part of me had started fantasizing about leaving because of it!

The very thing we so love about a person can also be what causes us to lose our minds.

Back then, I focused only on Alex's limitations. Now I know that my struggle to accept and tolerate our differences was more complicated than that. I, too, was limited, but in ways I was unwilling and unable to acknowledge then.

Instead of investing in my own abilities, I fired an emergency flare and started thinking that he and I weren't a good match. Instead of acknowledging my own role in our troubles,

I felt trapped. Trapped inside myself, trapped inside my own story, trapped inside my story of Alex, and unable to ask for more, unable to do anything about my fears.

Just as I had been in childhood: Powerless. Dissociated. And entirely alone.

In short? I was triggered.

Buckle Up, Love Will Trigger You

It hurts to love. It's like giving yourself to be flayed and knowing that at any moment the other person may just walk off with your skin.

—Susan Sontag

Love can be a roller-coaster ride of emotions. One minute you're on top of the world, thinking your partner is an angel sent from heaven, and the next minute you're plotting their demise. Don't worry. It's not because you or your partner is broken or you're destined for an unhealthy relationship. It's because love, dating, and all other relationships are majorly triggering.

If love hasn't already triggered you, buckle up, because it will.

Triggered, pissed off, outraged, rageful, livid, fucking livid (a fave)—when we feel treated unfairly, we may experience strong feelings and an intense need to react. But most of the time, in those moments, reactivity is the last thing we need. Nothing is as urgent as it feels. I promise.

If you attempt to manage your relationships from a place of reactivity and urgency, you're likely to respond in ways that create conflict, distance, and disconnection. This is because our brain's fight, flight, or freeze response becomes activated, often misinterpreting situations and resulting in unnecessary chaos and unwanted drama.

When these emergency response systems take control, we lose our full agency, regardless of our intellect or rational capabilities. According to John Gottman, this chronic physiological presence of an emergency response is referred to as being "flooded." They explain, "Flooding predicts that our shields will go up, because we feel overwhelmed and either want to flee or immediately vanquish our partner's negativity." They identify three distinct aspects of flooding: "The first part is the shock of feeling attacked, blamed, and abandoned. The second part is awareness that we can't calm down. The third part is emotional shutdown." In essence, our minds and bodies perceive danger even when there isn't any actual threat. Consequently, we often act against our best interests, compelled to defend and protect ourselves.

Peter Levine calls this the "veracity trap," where he explains, "the more intense an emotion of fear or anger, the more we are hardwired to presume our assessment of threat to be true, that is, to be a real danger we must react to—full out—with our basic survival responses. In other words, *we equate veracity with emotional intensity.*" Reaching a state of internal flooding and subsequently assuming the absolute truth of such an experience is deeply rooted in our bodily responses. It pertains to how our bodies store trauma, giving rise to invisible wounds that are often triggered by our partners, leading us to feel flooded.

DEFINING TRIGGERS

Triggers are specific situations in the here and now that elicit powerful emotional responses rooted in wounds from past traumas.

But triggers don't produce just any emotional reaction. They can set off tremendous emotional upheaval that leads to frustration, contempt, and dysregulation. They are the urgent catastrophe created by an all-or-nothing, black-or-white perspective.

When an event or situation sparks a memory, it triggers your emotions. This is manifested chemically within your body—be it through hormones, neurotransmitters, or activation of the central nervous system. The memory being triggered doesn't have to be something you're actively aware of. Instead, it can surface abruptly as a potent emotional reaction, accompanied by a flurry of thoughts seemingly relevant only to the current situation. However, these powerful emotions are often linked to a deeper narrative from your past. This doesn't diminish the significance of the present moment, but it does shed light on why reactions can feel overwhelmingly intense. I often remind my clients that, when they're triggered, their emotional reactions are approximately 30 percent in response to the present situation and about 70 percent are tied to their past experiences—most commonly, trauma.

Let's go into this a bit more.

UNPACKING TRAUMA

Trauma is trending these days. *Finally*, there is no more minimizing or dismissing the impacts of trauma, no more "Suck it up" or "It's not a big deal" or "Other people have it worse."

It's crucial to emphasize the significance and depth of the world's wounds. Throughout history, humanity endured horrible traumas, all largely without addressing the profound impact they left in their wake. War, enslavement, genocide—these events weren't just small moments in our collective past; they shaped entire communities, cultures, and individual lives in myriad ways, and will continue to do so for generations. So, too, with generational family trauma. We are long overdue for deep, meaningful conversations around such trauma, and acknowledgment of its far-reaching repercussions.

But what is trauma? Who has experienced trauma? And what do we do about it?

Trauma is widespread. Hungarian Canadian physician Gabor Maté suggests (and I totally agree), "Someone without the marks of trauma would be an outlier in our society."

Trauma is often associated with specific events, particularly those involving physical or sexual abuse. While such experiences certainly qualify as significant trauma, trauma can also manifest in many other forms and at greater magnitudes. Some people may experience implicit or passive forms of abuse, such as a lack of necessary nurture, affection, guidance, or attention during childhood. Emotional abandonment and neglect also fall into this category.

Even those who didn't experience abuse in their childhood still went through the inherent difficulties of childhood, which in and of themselves can be a frightening experience. During our childhood, our parents hold significant power and influence over us. Michael Bader has said, "Parents have the authority to define reality." They shape our entire being through both implicit and explicit teaching, modeling their behavior and attitudes for us.

When we think of trauma or abuse, we often focus on what was done to us. But what is just as important is what was *not* done, *not* provided, *not* allowed for. Psychologist Stephen Mitchell has said, "The terrible destructiveness of childhood abuse lies not just in the trauma of what happens but also in the tragic loss of what is not provided—a protected space for psychological growth."

Therapist Terry Real calls this "passive abuse," and it is prevalent in many families that lack warmth, affirmation, and emotional or intellectual nurturing. Emotional detachment, distance, and lack of connection can have detrimental effects on a growing child or teen, but these effects are often overlooked. "You don't remember trauma," Real says. "You relive it."

Gabor Maté goes as far as to say that our early traumas "dictate much of our behavior, shape our social habits, and inform our ways of thinking about the world." This fits with what we know now about how trauma affects development and how people work as adults.

Bessel van der Kolk, author of *The Body Keeps the Score*, offers profound insights into the impacts of trauma. He states, "We have learned that trauma is not just an event that took place sometime in the past; it is also the imprint left by that experience on mind, brain, and body. This imprint has ongoing consequences for how the human organism manages to survive in the present. Trauma results in a fundamental reorganization of the way the mind and brain manage perceptions. It changes not only how we think and what we think about, but also our very capacity to think."

Trauma experienced during childhood and adolescence will undeniably shape how you cope with subsequent life challenges throughout adulthood, maybe even for the rest of your life. The framework that trauma creates will be particularly relevant to our adult partnerships as their structure and centrality to our lives directly parallel our early attachment relationships. That is why some say that all relationships are formed in part by who we've become or who we want to become as a result of trauma.

Peter Levine, known for his Somatic Experiencing approach to trauma, refers to the impacts of trauma as "the tyranny of the past." He goes on to explain how trauma "can alter a person's biological, psychological, and social equilibrium to such a degree that the memory of one particular event comes to taint and dominate all other experiences, spoiling an appreciation of the present moment."

Our partner might say goodbye to us in a certain tone of voice, and we believe they're about to abandon us. They might forget to respond to a text, and we believe the very worst is about to happen. They might decline sex, and it feels like a full-body, all-encompassing rejection, even if they fucked you for five hours the day before. All these can be considered triggers, and with these triggers, something in the moment is colored with hues from our past, and we become stuck, able to see our present reality only through the lens of our past fears. Then we react in the same manner as we did during childhood. We might become depressed, shut down, withdraw, or spiral into a place of hopelessness. We may even become dysregulated and experience a sense of being out of control. We can obsess and become hypervigilant and pre-occupied. By contrast, some people might react to a trigger in the opposite way they did as a child and turn their feelings of powerlessness into aggression or anger. The underlying message, regardless of the response, is the same: I need to defend and protect myself. Over time, all these reactions become ingrained and, consequently, shape our perceptions and experiences well into our adult lives.

Therapeutic approaches have provided a new language with which to better understand trauma, triggers, and types of conflict. "Attachment styles" have been placed front and center in discussions of relationships. "Inner child" and re-parenting work, in which the aim is for individuals to provide the love and nurturing to themselves that was absent in child-hood, has also become popular. And the Internal Family Systems (IFS) model of therapy looks at the self as being made up of a team of parts, like a family living inside you, each member with their own role, emotional experiences, and coping mechanisms. Another, unattributed approach divides our reactivity into two groups: adaptive child and competent adult.

Even though I like all these theories, I don't think you can rely on just one; each offers valuable insights. Integrating them alongside thought from other fields, like sociology and cultural studies, will provide a much more comprehensive understanding of the complex nature of our relational experiences.

But let's simplify things.

When we enter a relationship, we fundamentally become dependent upon the other person. In that space, we have a lot to lose. It's risky, and we are in a position of vulnerability. This dependence parallels our attachments to and relationships with our early caregivers. As a result, powerful triggers in our present will be deeply rooted in our history.

The way we respond to those triggers gives us valuable insight into our past experiences and how they shaped who we are. Consider a trigger to be a revelation, an opportunity to remember or learn something important about yourself that was previously hidden.

One big lesson to learn is this: Our reaction to triggers may have worked for us in the past, but they likely will not serve us well in the present. The more aware of this we are, the better we can address our concerns, get our needs met, and feel more satisfied. All traumas are relational and will shape all of our subsequent experiences with connection, intimacy, and trust. These early experiences become a blueprint for how we approach others and how we understand ourselves.

THE RE-ENACTMENT

Every relationship—with a lover, long-term partner, friend, or co-worker—has its own dance, which is shaped by the present and has roots in childhood. Love, communication, self-esteem, insecurity, and conflict avoidance are all learned and repeated. Whether we are on a first date or celebrating our twenty-year anniversary, we all re-enact, repeat, and seek out what is familiar.

Resist viewing re-enactment through a negative lens. Many people spiral and talk about their "unhealthy patterns," but patterns are simply re-enactments that offer us the opportunity to repair and heal. And each time a different, more healthful choice can be made. If you're open to it.

The word *re-enactment* is not as widely discussed on social media as *trauma* or *trigger*, but it's just as important. (Listen up: This is going to transform how you think about yourself and all your relationships.) A re-enactment is an unconscious process by which we re-create patterns, dynamics, or unresolved issues. Every re-enactment involves varying degrees of a re-creation of familiar roles, emotions, thoughts, and behaviors that lead to a variety of different relational dynamics. These dynamics impact everything from communication, to patterns of attachment, to love-seeking behaviors, to confidence, and even to sexual preferences. Re-enactments are normal and should be expected. Many therapists and theorists see purpose to each re-enactment. Sigmund Freud coined the term *repetition compulsion*, which suggests that re-enactments are attempts to gain mastery or resolution over unresolved childhood issues.

Unfortunately, there's no nasal swab or blood test to pinpoint why we re-enact patterns in our lives. But understanding the "why" isn't as crucial as gaining awareness of the patterns in the first place. By becoming more conscious of them, we can avoid the ones that lead to disconnection and other negative outcomes.

Re-enactments are so deep (and can be so hidden) within

relational dynamics that they can create the context for most relationships without our realizing it. The person we're dating or are madly in love with can trigger terminal feelings of being disappointed, abandoned, unwanted, or viciously judged. There is both a very real relational dynamic we're responding to in the present (usually) and a re-enactment of an earlier, past dynamic.

"I DON'T HAVE ISSUES WITH ANYONE ELSE IN MY LIFE"

This is what my clients tell me about the challenges they face with their partner. And this is what Alex said to me. I always responded, "Of course the person with whom you have the biggest challenges is your partner!"

Our partners play a very important, often central, role in our lives. We might live with them, rely on them, and share things with them that we don't share with anyone else. Our partner's flaws therefore significantly affect our lives unlike anyone else's. If a friend lets us down, we might find it easier to get past it, but when our partner disappoints us it could make us rethink the whole relationship. It is only our adult partnerships that directly parallel our early attachment relationships. This is why similar issues will arise.

Things We All Do in Extraordinary Ways

• We actively choose and even seek out partners who will love us in ways that feel familiar. Yes, the person you're dating is, in one way or another, symbolic of your experiences from childhood.

- We co-create a dynamic that resembles a re-enactment of our earlier experiences and that will leave us feeling something very familiar.
- We feel entitled to a variety of things from our partner to make those feelings go away.

I see each re-enactment as an unconscious chance to regain control of something that was once painful, intolerable, or absent. It's about gaining power, not over that thing, but from within. In re-enacting a past pattern, we unconsciously re-create a dynamic that allows us to do something different and to transform.

Ultimately, we are the ones in the driver's seat. We decide how long we will acquiesce and if and when we need to pull away. We are, in fact, the ones co-writing the relational script. If we want to make any changes or edits, we can do it. If we're dating someone, and they are horrible at texting or don't share in the effort to schedule dates, we can ask for more or decide to end it.

We can deal with these things from our childhood in the context of our relationships as adults by changing who we are. The key is: We have to be open to it. Most people find it hard to do this because they have built up a whole set of mental defenses to keep them from confronting past losses. This is what we therapists call resistance.

My clients always want to know, "Is it my partner or my past?" And the answer is: It's both. It's a combination of your childhood issues and your partner. Don't make the mistake of boiling down the complexity of how you and your partner interact to just one thing or one person. There is always much more to the story.

ALEX AND ME: WHEN LOVE TRIGGERS YOU

With Alex, I was being triggered and didn't even realize it (or want to admit it).

In triggering moments, it can be helpful to make lists to identify patterns. With a list written down in black and white, your unconscious becomes conscious. Because most of our thoughts and feelings are complex, it is important to take a look at them when they arise. You don't have to analyze each and every variation in your thoughts and feelings, but be aware that there is always a story behind your conscious awareness in the here and now.

My Responsive Themes to Triggers
- Withdrawal
- Silence
- Disgust and contempt
- Retreat to my internal world
- Dissociation

Notice how all these protective responses point to the presence of a frightened child doing everything they can to hide. They convey an unconscious of "I'm scared that if I speak, I will get punished, abandoned, or rejected."

Unconsciously, my body was saying, "I'm scared."

My reactions were not engaging, assertive, or productive. They did not show any signs of my being emotionally or physically present, being an adult in control of the situation. I didn't fight. I didn't provide feedback. I didn't criticize. I simply retreated into an internal world that was safe, controllable, and fundamentally disconnected. In other words, I checked all the way out.

This dissociation was caused by the same sense of powerlessness and hopelessness I had learned during childhood. Growing up, I was not encouraged or allowed to make decisions for myself. As the youngest, my opinions and experiences were often criticized by my family, which undermined my autonomy and self-confidence. I was perceived as knowing very little, someone who shouldn't be taken seriously, and someone to blame. As a result, I internalized this role and struggled to trust my own judgment and decision-making abilities and remained in a silent paralyzed state. This was particularly evident in my withdrawal from Alex: It was in withdrawing that I silenced myself just like I learned in childhood.

Silence, I believed, was the safest place I could be.

My present fears were based upon (big) assumptions about who Alex was. My main issue was his lack of psychological depth; he had little access to self-awareness or insight, which in turn served as a barrier to communication and understanding. At least, that's how *I* saw it. No one in my family had ever shared their feelings. Instead, they enacted them behaviorally, just as Alex did. They'd use a shift in their tone of voice, withdrawal, yelling, emotional distance, and passive-aggressive expressions of "I'm mad"—when what they were actually trying to communicate (and what would have been out of the question for them to say) was "I'm sad."

I was sometimes triggered by the way Alex spoke—at times, he would raise his voice; he wasn't screaming at me, but he would get flustered easily, at me or anything, really—and it would push me over the edge. In response, I would sit silently in disgust. I wasn't even aware I was doing this. But my reactions always led down the road of disconnection and loneliness.

It's easy to stay focused on the trigger, the here and now,

but what's more helpful is, instead, to think about the outcome of your *response* to that trigger. The result of my withdrawal—regardless of the reason—was loneliness; when I shut down, I also shut Alex out, which only deepened my loneliness and made me sad. This was a re-enactment, and it was all I knew.

Ultimately, I was anxious—just as you are—about the long-term viability of our relationship. Could I see myself with Alex forever? I wanted kids and tried to envision working through co-parenting conflicts with him. Immediately, I saw flashing lights. I saw a replay of my parents fighting about their contrasting parenting styles. I saw Alex and me doing the same thing they had done. And I absolutely did not want to put a child through that. *Not this again*, my unconscious said.

As Lacanian psychologist Annie Rogers writes in *The Unsayable*, "The unconscious insists, repeats, and practically breaks down the door, to be heard." My unconscious mind was speaking loudly to me . . . but in a complex narrative I wasn't listening to.

My withdrawal had been triggered by a conscious narrative that went something like this: *It's hopeless. I don't want to be with someone who can't control himself or communicate like an adult.* What I didn't realize at the time was that this narrative of contempt was also a form of hypervigilance, one that kept me on high alert for potential danger, hurt, or loss. If I had had the capacity for complex thought and understanding during childhood, those are the words I would have used to describe the threatening and hurtful experience with my family, too.

Understanding this concept is crucial. As adults, we have a broader understanding, more emotional insight, and a higher level of awareness compared to when we are children. Often, the things we say to our partners are the things we wish we could have expressed to our parents or caregivers when we were young but never felt safe enough to say.

My father's entire personality was one big aggressive temper tantrum. As a child, I found this terrifying. If I could go back to childhood and react to him instead with insight and emotion, I would have said to him, "I don't want a father who can't control his anger. I feel unsafe when you're angry."

In my relationship with Alex, I was picking up on major differences that needed to be addressed, negotiated, and either resolved or tolerated and accepted. However, my triggered mind created a defensive strategy that shut down my capacity to engage and, therefore, had a deep impact on the relationship. Morally, I was convinced that I was "right," a terrible word to use in the relationship realm. Because if I was right, then Alex was wrong. Feeling right was the only way I was able to feel confident and powerful. If Alex was bad, then I was good. Another horribly ineffective approach to the relational challenge—and a brand of self-righteousness I see in most of the couples I counsel.

At the time, I of course wasn't aware of these thoughts or what was actually happening. It was only after years of reflection that I gained a better understanding. My silence reflected the many ways in which I had struggled to feel powerful, confident, and secure enough to push, challenge, and confront—in productive ways—in order to elicit a different reaction from Alex. I responded to my father's anger with withdrawal and feelings of powerlessness because talking to him was not an option; if I had, his anger would have escalated, and I would have been punished and felt rejected and alone. As a child, this behavior was adaptive for my safety, but as an adult, especially in my relationship with Alex, it was entirely different; speaking up and expressing myself was not only safe but essential. But I faltered because I was so triggered and everything I did was influenced by the responses I had learned through my childhood trauma.

I couldn't do anything about how awful my family was. They simply didn't understand me, and they treated me as if I spoke another language. I learned early on that when I confronted or responded to this mistreatment, it would only harden my father's abusive stance. He would yell louder, and in the end, I would have to apologize to him.

His famous line was "I'm the dictator, and you have to listen to me." I'm not kidding—he frequently referred to himself as the family dictator without any awareness of how ridiculous he sounded. And no one said anything to contradict him. There was no changing him.

My mother just told me to stay quiet. "He's a sick man," she would say. And he was. My brothers would tell me to just deal with it. The message was clear: Stay quiet, take the abuse, and just wait until you can leave. So, for years, I followed the rules. When he yelled at me, I turned off, dissociated, and waited for him to finish.

And I did the exact same thing with Alex in response to my own dissatisfaction. For years, I never actually confronted or pushed him or tried to change the relationship. I talked about it with everyone—friends, family, my therapist, and my journal—over and over. The one person I didn't talk about it with was Alex. I didn't tell him about my anxieties, or about how my satisfaction had been plummeting. I was convinced that he had a limited capacity to process such information, to work on things. The truth was, I also had a limited capacity to change. My withdrawal was a symptom of a scared inner child who felt powerless. I, too, was unwilling to change, and my expectation that *he* should was completely unrealistic.

We were both limited. We were both re-creating dynamics from our childhoods. Unfortunately, neither of us was able to effectively communicate this or understand it.

Love triggered me. It felt lacking, and I didn't know what to do but feel hopeless. During this period, Derek was giving me the insights and the tools, but I still didn't do any work to try to change the situation. I was paralyzed with anxiety. I didn't want to end the relationship; I loved Alex. But I also didn't necessarily want to be in the relationship, either, because of how hopeless I felt about anything's ever changing. I was so triggered that not only was I unable to differentiate a trigger from reality, but it also became harder for me to accept Alex for who he was or to enjoy the good qualities he had to offer.

Derek would try to shift the conversation away from my experience of Alex's limitations and toward my family history. I didn't like that. I didn't want to look at myself. Alex had triggered me, and I felt righteously entitled to my feelings. And my reactions *were* valid: Alex *was* limited. My experience *was* real. Yet, my reactions to his shortcomings were skewing my perception of him, myself, indeed, the whole world and universe.

Certainly, this overwhelming influence wasn't solely because Alex didn't directly communicate his emotions . . .

The point to remember here is that when there's conflict it's always about *both* of you. Both you and your partner. It may sound strange but there is only so much we can be sure of. Yes, we should do our best to understand ourselves, and share this with our partner. But even then, there's always going to be a level of uncertainty in any relationship. This unknown factor isn't just a part of relationships; it actually defines them.

Prolific researcher John Gottman astutely wrote, "No one is right. There is no absolute reality in marital conflict, only two subjective ones." Terry Real similarly emphasizes the point when he says, "There is no place for objective reality in personal relationships." Both Real and Gottman get at a crucial point, one we must accept if we're to engage in healthy and compassionate relationships. Real continues: "It's never a matter of two people landing on the one true reality, but rather of negotiating differing subjective realities."

The point is, there is no place for "truth" or "rightness" in a relationship. Relational dynamics produce emotions. And emotions aren't a question of right or wrong. They are a question of understanding and meaning. They stand in for a story.

My shutdown with Alex was a direct response to very real things; I wasn't making them up.

Most of us have reactions or responses in our relationships to very real dynamics. Whether the reaction is anxiety, dissociation, depression, or any other emotional or defensive response, it is *responsive*. Something in the present has triggered that response. It's not a hallucination; it *is* happening. But the power or largeness of the emotions we feel isn't about your partner. While your partner may have triggered you, the emotional response is yours to own.

The mindfuck of it all is that, often, the way we respond to real disappointment ends up eliciting further disappointment. Again, we elicit the very reaction we're trying to avoid. For example, most people, when disappointed, will respond in critical or even demeaning ways. "You didn't do X for me, and it's proof that you suck"—a response that would make anyone defensive or want to run away.

IMPORTANT CAVEAT

Many things are sold as being all about childhood. Yes, and no. As usual, there is a lot more to the story. It's about what happened, what didn't happen, and what subsequently prevented access to healing. It's about the defense mechanisms we develop in the face of trauma and then cling to as our value system in order to avoid danger. We must perform the herculean task of holding multiple truths at the same time while also having empathy for both our partner and ourselves. This is why we say relationships are hard work.

Sometimes we (or our partners) can act like jerks. Sometimes we (or our partners) are actually mistreated. Even if our partner's behavior triggers emotional reactivity in us, that's no reason not to react. React, take space if you're being mistreated, and then reflect and seek understanding after the fact.

Not all triggers are bad. Some heal.

A corrective emotional experience is an experience in the present that helps counteract and even reshape the beliefs and emotions that originated from past traumas. It's an opportunity for reframing and healing. The concept of a corrective emotional experience is often discussed in the context of the therapist relationship. I believe it is applicable to any relationship, especially those with our adult partners. One particular corrective experience with Alex stands out in my memory.

There was a period when Alex and I shared a car, *his* car. One day, while we were out looking at vintage furniture, I pulled the car out of a parking spot and hit a pole. The front fender fell off. I was in a state of panic. I thought for sure Alex was going to yell at me, hold the accident over me, be passive-aggressive for months, but . . . he seemed unbothered.

I didn't believe him and I apologized profusely—over and over, for the rest of the day.

Dropping him off at our place, I sped off to "run some errands." At an auto parts store, I bought adhesive, car paint, and other items I couldn't tell you the names of. (I can't believe I actually thought I could do auto body work! Talk about fight or flight!) Back home, I worked on the detached fender in the garage for about thirty minutes. When Alex walked in, he found me on my knees, sweating and in a complete meltdown.

"Babe! What are you doing? What's wrong? It's okay."

I wasn't convinced. "It's not okay. This is a big deal. I fucked up your car."

"Todd, I truthfully don't care. We'll bring it to a repair shop, it'll be fixed, and that will be that. This stuff happens. Also, you can barely change a lightbulb, and all of a sudden you know how to fix a car fender?" He cackled cutely and pulled me up to meet him at eye level. He gave me a big kiss, hugged me, and said, "It's *okaaaaay*, okay?"

Then we fucked on the car hood (which most likely caused more dents).

When I was younger, my father screamed and punished me for all mistakes, from breaking a glass and overflowing the toilet to that time I actually totaled my parents' car. And with Alex's car, my entire being had thought Alex was going to do the same.

Our triggers can certainly cause reactive conflict. But they can also be important lessons. At that moment, I was convinced that Alex was going to react the way my father used to: scream, hurt me, and basically reject or abandon me. But he didn't. This is part of how we can heal in the context of a safe adult relationship.

When we experience things that challenge our fears, our brains form new neural pathways, a powerful and effective way of promoting healing. Repeated exposure to these reparative experiences creates change. After the fender experience, I no longer feared the consequences (getting abused) of breaking things.

Many people who had difficult childhoods struggle to receive love and special care as adults. I know I definitely did. And this was one big thing I learned from being with Alex. I learned how to receive love even when I had messed up.

Our triggers teach us about ourselves; they show us where our soft spots are, where we might turn to give ourselves a little love and to ask for it from our partners.

DENISE AND SAM: DOUBLE TRAUMA

Denise, a thirty-nine-year-old bisexual Canadian American cisgender woman, and Sam, a forty-five-year-old heterosexual cisgender white male, were clients of mine for two years. Despite having been together for nearly a decade, both Denise and Sam had experienced significant abuse and trauma during their childhood and adolescence. While it was heart-wrenching to listen to their painful experiences, what stood out for me was their impressive resilience and the genuine care they showed for each other during our sessions.

As therapists, it's our responsibility to be attuned to such dynamics. What happens in session usually is what happens out of session, and some couples who sit in front of me are actively cruel to each other. But I sensed a deep, caring connection between Denise and Sam. Still, while they demonstrated care and compassion, they were also both shut down to the point of dissociation. Their past traumas had continued to haunt them (as they often do), preventing them from fully embracing or being able to relax into the love and warmth already present in their relationship.

Denise and Sam had certainly faced unique challenges, but what made their situation most difficult was the way they responded to triggers, ultimately causing a cycle of triggering each other. Whenever Denise felt triggered, she would withdraw, become silent, and dissociate from her surroundings, essentially shutting down. Her body would go into survival mode, preparing to flee. As she pulled away, Sam would feel abandoned (as he had felt in childhood), anxious, and resentful. This caused him to pursue Denise for attention and reassurance. This wasn't because he didn't respect her boundaries but because his own dysregulation made it difficult for him to control his behavior and recognize that Denise needed space, not pursuit. Unfortunately, the inability of both to regulate their emotions only made things worse; it became hard for them to repair things after a conflict, to have sex, or even just to plan fun outings together. It seemed that each was stuck in the defensive position they had learned in childhood to cope with their traumas.

During our therapy sessions, we dedicated a significant amount of time to exploring and processing their trauma, while also prioritizing the development of empathy and understanding in both. It's crucial that each partner have a basic understanding of the other's triggers and trauma in order to avoid emotional land mines in the relationship. With Denise and Sam, after we had processed both their past traumas, we shifted our focus to creating a narrative that helped them make sense of their past and explore ways to move forward in the present.

However, their emotional reactivity often hindered their ability to fully appreciate the positive aspects of the relationship, presenting a significant obstacle to their progress. Neither Denise nor Sam had ever been able to safely relax into a relationship, let alone receive love without fear of abuse. Realizing this became a turning point for both of them. They started to create a warm and caring environment for each other, something they both desperately needed in order to heal from their past traumas. By allowing themselves to receive love and to trust in the positive aspects of their relationship, they were finally able to begin the process of healing.

Like Denise and Sam, for many of us the idea of feeling emotionally safe and secure in an intimate relationship can seem foreign, even unsettling. As a child, I learned to associate disappointment with threat or danger, and those experiences continue to shape my understanding of relationships. Whether it's the fear of abandonment, the pain of rejection, or the trauma of abuse, these experiences can trigger defensive responses in us, even in the face of a caring and supportive partner. While it's important to process our trauma and pain, we often overlook the importance of moving forward toward pleasure, joy, and connection.

Recovering from trauma isn't about just processing it and making peace with it. It's about learning how to live again without fear. This is why it is crucial to recognize not only what occurred during trauma but also what did not. Often, it's what

did *not* occur—for example, the fostering of safety and trust—
that we find hardest to accept.

Many people who've been through trauma often stay in a
state of high alert. We pay a lot of attention to these fears and
the constant hypervigilance, which can be debilitating, but we
don't pay enough attention to the need for pleasure, joy, relaxation, and a sense of ease. These calming experiences create a
sense of safety. And it is safety that often is absent in the presence of trauma.

7

How to Grow Up

Human beings seem to have an almost unlimited capacity to deceive themselves, and to deceive themselves into taking their own lies for truth.

—R. D. LAING

A mid the complexities of this modern life, many of us are disconnected from our inner selves; we are fearful and avoidant of being honest with ourselves, reluctant to voice our thoughts, and overly concerned with the lives of others. We've become uncertain of our desires, our goals, and the means with which to achieve them, thus obscuring the pathway toward fulfillment. Instead, we look outward—toward partners, family, or even strangers online—hoping to find a sense of purpose, belonging, and acceptance that we've been unable to find within. In essence, we are seeking rescue from others. Yet, beneath this external search lies a profound sense of being adrift, an inability to fully embrace one's true self, and a persistent fear of the consequences of vulnerability.

In this pursuit for acceptance and fulfillment, these dynamics significantly influence our relationships. Whether single, dating, or in a committed relationship, we often become engrossed in analyzing others rather than focusing on ourselves. We will ask questions like:

Why haven't they responded?
Why can't they just do the laundry, like I asked?
Why can't they express their feelings to me openly?
Are they losing interest in me?
Do they still find me attractive?
Why are they so distant?
Are they keeping something from me?
Will they reject me if I bring up this conversation?
    Should I even bring it up?

We analyze others to avoid being honest with ourselves. This defense mechanism helps us manage our anxiety and fear, but in the process, we subtly distance ourselves from our personal experiences, which enables us to sidestep or further suppress the discomfort our questions about our partner may imply. In this way, we find ourselves ensnared in a cycle of assuming, forecasting, and obsessively attempting to comprehend the other person, all the while avoiding genuine dialogue. This way is safer, as by focusing primarily on others, we avoid having to confront the pain, sorrow, and loss embedded within our own psyche.

Ignoring, avoiding, and repressing oneself will never end well. Bessel van der Kolk writes, "As long as you keep secrets and suppress information, you are fundamentally at war with yourself . . . The critical issue is allowing yourself to know what you know. That takes an enormous amount of courage." Van der Kolk gets at a critical point: the importance of being self-aware and acknowledging hard truths in order to grow.

We all play a role in defining the conditions of our relationships. Even if our role is to be silent or passive, or to stay in the relationship while feeling deeply unsatisfied, it's still a role. But:

When we chronically avoid facing conflict and withhold our true feelings or concerns, our unresolved resentment can grow into something larger and unmanageable.

When we express our disappointment through criticism, we tend to elicit defensiveness and guarantee that our needs will go unfulfilled.

When we monopolize the conversation with our own thoughts and feelings, without also holding space for our partner, we inadvertently end up pushing our partner away.

When we complain about our partner's not expressing enough interest in us but refuse to self-disclose, we make ourselves invisible.

Perhaps it might not be these scenarios you find yourself in, but rest assured, we all play some role in defining our relationship. And don't for a second confuse this with blame. Again, we're all flawed and imperfect. We all end up with a partner who triggers us, who puts us face-to-face with some of our unfinished business. We all have problems! Face them! Honor them! Laugh at them. But also understand them.

If your goal is to increase overall relational satisfaction and daily well-being (and yes, that is the goal), the best way to seek change is from within. James Hollis wrote, "The best thing we can do for our relationship with others . . . is to render our relationship to ourselves more conscious." Similarly, Stephen Levine and his wife, author Ondrea Levine, wrote, "The distance from your pain, your grief, your unattended wounds, is the distance from your partner." Their words highlight how important it is to foster a conscious connection with ourselves if we are to have satisfying and connected relationships.

But this is easier said than done. During an initial session with a couple, one or both partners might express a desire for me to change the other. "Here is my partner. Here are the reasons they suck. Change them, or I'm out." The one partner blames the other for their own emotions, saying, "You made me feel _____."

Similarly, when I work with a single client, a substantial part of our initial session tends to be spent exploring the narrative constructed around a potential partner, a narrative based largely on the client's interpretations and assumptions drawn from a few dates or text messages. "They didn't text me back until five hours later. If they were interested, wouldn't they have responded sooner?"

Both these common complaints overlook a fundamental truth about relationships: The feelings that surface within our interactions are a reaction to an experience that we played a role in shaping. The spotlight can't solely be on the other person. Indeed, your partner doesn't "make" you feel a certain way. And if you're frustrated by the person you're dating because of their lack of responsiveness, not addressing those concerns with that person will guarantee that nothing will change, even if the change required is disengagement.

These approaches reflect misplacement of the responsibility for personal happiness, suggesting that our satisfaction is dependent on another person. The common expectation is for the other person to change or provide us with something that will make us feel accepted, improved, or happier or that will ease our discomfort. However, few people acknowledge their own contribution to these unfulfilling dynamics.

This habit of blame and contempt, whether directed inwardly or outwardly, becomes a zero-sum game, leaving each person feeling powerless.

This is what I did. (Oopsie!) And it's why I felt confused and trapped.

EVERYONE LOSES IN THE BLAME GAME

I was convinced that everything was Alex's fault. In order for me to be happy, in order for our relationship to improve, *he* needed to change.

But what about my voice? Why didn't I use it?

I was young, had never lived on my own, and was still recovering from the horrors of my childhood, which had taught me to be small and powerless. When I entered this relationship, I let myself become defined by it. At the beginning, this worked. But over time, it became clear that something needed to change, and I, as the perfect little angel, figured it was Alex who needed to make that change. Not me. Not the entire structure of our relationship. Not the fact that we had no life outside the relationship. Not the fact that we never truly talked about our needs or expectations.

I was doing what every person in a couple I've ever seen does: I was spending more time trying to change my partner than trying to change myself—not because of Alex's limitations but because of my *understanding* of his limitations, because of the story I told myself about who he was, what I needed, and why his not making a change would be detrimental to my future—to my unborn children, even.

My perspective informed the role I assumed and the stance I took with Alex. It was the same physical and emotional stance I had taken in childhood to cope with and protect myself from the scary reality I was living. But the more I withdrew, the more silent I became, the more Alex would ignore my emotions—because I wasn't sharing them with him! The less I asked of Alex, the less aware he was of what he was supposed to try harder to give me. And what was the result? You guessed it. I felt unseen, unheard, and invisible.

My perspective at the time was that if he didn't ask I wasn't going to share. And because he didn't ask, that meant he didn't care in the way I needed him to. I assumed he should just *know* to ask, should just *know* to do certain things and not others. For me, if I had to ask for something from him in order to get it, that thing wasn't worth asking for. I thought he should just give it to me without prompting. The reality was I felt invisible because I had *made* myself invisible. I projected onto Alex the unresolved expectations and disappointments from my childhood. I was searching for the validation, acceptance, and care I had never gotten from my parents.

STOP BEING MEAN TO YOURSELF

From my experience with clients, friends, and virtually everyone I've come across, it's clear that people aren't just tough on themselves; they can be downright harsh. If we are ever to grow, it's crucial to address this promptly and adopt a more compassionate, softer approach toward oneself.

You can hold yourself accountable while still holding yourself in high regard. You can understand your flaws *and* still honor your own humanity. Admitting that you play a role in your relationship is a necessary strength.

So, *stop being mean to yourself*. As a kid, I was an expert self-beater-upper. As a child, I learned to be insecure and developed low self-esteem. I would use any mistake or flaw as a weapon to reinforce these beliefs. When I told Derek this, his response was "Todd, don't even go there. This isn't true. This is your father speaking." After a while, I started to talk back to the negative voice in my head, telling myself, *Do not go there*. It's what I tell my clients, and it's what I will tell you now: Do not go there. It's a waste of time.

If you want to move on and improve your life, you cannot be mean to yourself, ever. (Yes, I've just said not to do something ever.) We all make mistakes. And if, when you feel shame, embarrassment, or guilt, you're convinced you're a terrible person, understand that *that is your childhood trauma speaking.* So, for now, don't go there, babe. You're wonderful and imperfect. Welcome to the club!

Now, back to being the powerful adult you are today.

If we want to impact our relationships in a positive way, we can't wait around for the other person to bring up the hard conversations, to make the plans, to return that text message, or to fulfill all our needs. This is what it means to be powerful and confident and to invest in your innate ability to make positive change in your relationships—something many of us simply weren't able to do as children.

I was convinced that Alex was the problem. He was great at communicating, staying in touch, and being present. This I loved. But when faced with a problem, he couldn't talk about how he felt, because he had so little self-awareness. He was emotionally immature—or so I thought. We had a completely different set of skills. I could, and wanted to, actively communicate my emotions, but he would regularly say, "I'm not one of your clients"—my father used to say (and I shit you not), "Stop talking to me like a textbook." It was the same messaging—or, at least, that's how I received it in the moment.

Derek always used to say, "Alex speaks in code." And he was right. Alex couldn't communicate his emotions as

I did mine, but he did communicate them in one way or another. When he told me he wasn't one of my clients, what he was actually saying was "I feel like you're judging me or trying to change me." While he could have welcomed the opportunity to change, it's also true that what I said to him was communicating criticism. I felt contemptuous of Alex's emotional limitations. And I *was* trying to change him; from my perspective, he needed to change. Alex was picking up on that criticism but was unable to respond to it in a helpful way because *I* was not communicating in a way that could be heard.

My relational house of cards fell because I was convinced that Alex was the problem. The story I told myself about him kept me from exploring alternative explanations. It stopped me from looking outside the box of bias that had defined my subjective experience.

It's important to recognize that the stories we tell ourselves about our partner are not necessarily based on reality but rather on our *perception* of reality. But our perception can become distorted by our own trauma, insecurities, and fears. That is why flexibility is so important in a relationship. Being able to change our perspective is one of the most important skills we can master for ourselves and our relationships.

I was not yet open to this idea, though. I was closed off and self-righteous, convinced that my perspective was the absolute truth. This kind of black-and-white thinking, this self-righteousness, is a definite red flag. If this is you, it's time for a big pause.

I was unknowingly self-sabotaging. My lack of accountability made me feel powerless to create any changes in my life.

Even if Alex had changed, it wouldn't have made a difference, because what I wanted from him was something that only *I* could give myself. I needed to take responsibility for my own agency and create the change I desired.

This is what it means to differentiate.

WHEN "TWO BECOME ONE"

A lack of differentiation can be likened to fusion, where two individuals become one. Psychiatrist Murray Bowen introduced the concept of differentiation to family systems theory in the 1950s, and it was later refined by therapist David Schnarch in the 1990s. In his work, Schnarch defines *differentiation* as the ability of individuals to agree (or disagree) without feeling like they're losing their sense of self. People who are well differentiated can handle disagreements without getting overwhelmed, resentful, or passive-aggressive. Even with significant differences in opinions or needs, these people can stay connected to their partners.

Differentiation starts in our family of origin throughout childhood and adolescence, as we form our own identities separate from those of our family. We develop our own beliefs, values, and interests, which may be different from those of our family members. Ideally, our parents will help us during this transformation. They will nurture our independence, offering encouraging words and actions that support us while we safely explore our new developing sense of self.

In many families, the reality is far from ideal. In families like mine (and perhaps yours), support and nurturance often came at the cost of self-sacrifice. Independence and self-exploration were either discouraged or, in extreme cases, harshly punished. This kind of parenting teaches a child that self-expression will be accompanied by threat and is, therefore, unsafe. As a result, many of us adopt a feeling of powerlessness in our relationships. We learn that safety is found in conformity and in silencing our own voices, rather than in being authentically ourselves and accepted as we are. In pop psychology, this disconnection from one's self is known as self-loss.

Schnarch uses an analogy I love: The differentiated couple is not in one boat together, but in two separate boats that are navigating the waters independently but alongside each other. For this couple, Schnarch says, "It's about getting closer and more distinct—rather than more distant." In this way, Schnarch would argue (as would I) that the ideal approach to our partner aligns with Erich Fromm's perspective, which emphasizes, "I want the loved person to grow and unfold for his own sake, and in his own ways, and not for the purpose of serving me." Esther Perel reflects on something similar and writes, "When two become one, connection can no longer happen. There is no one to connect with."

We are individuals, each with our unique identities and interests. As paradoxical as it might sound, taking time apart can actually bring a couple closer together. It allows for personal growth, which in turn enhances the collective growth of the relationship. So, yes, being apart, having your own space and activities, is a necessary ingredient for being together, for deepening intimacy, and for maintaining a healthy, balanced relationship.

Ultimately, a differentiated relationship is a delicate dance between "me" time and "us" time. It's about balancing individual growth with shared experiences, about fostering mutual respect for personal space while also nurturing the intimacy holding the relationship together.

This was a major problem for me and Alex. And it is one of the most common issues I see with the couples I treat.

At first glance, all this might seem straightforward. You might think, *I'm independent, I have a strong voice, and I lead my own life. My partner and I are separate individuals.* And in many ways, you probably are. Yet, true differentiation goes much deeper. It's intricate, demanding both the acknowledgment of internal dissonance and external conflict and a strategy for handling that conflict.

Derek calls this emotional karate. I call it mission: impossible. Remember the scene in *Mission: Impossible* where Tom Cruise is trying to avoid the laser alarm system? One wrong step, and the alarm is triggered.

I want to share with you a story about Mark and Bianca, who grappled with issues of differentiation requiring big change. Their struggles were deeply rooted in their family histories. Neither Mark nor Bianca had ever truly confronted the challenges of their childhoods, and so they found themselves doing so in adulthood, with each other. Their story further underscores the intricate ties between our families of origin and the relationships we create in adulthood.

MARK AND BIANCA: A HEADACHE IS SAFER THAN HEARTACHE

Mark, a forty-eight-year-old straight cisgender white male, and Bianca, a forty-two-year-old pansexual, cisgender white female, entered therapy as a "high-conflict" couple. (Some couples present high conflict, while others are "conflict avoidant."

Mark and Bianca were higher than high.) When we describe high-conflict couples, I like to think of their unyielding conflict as a method of connection, even though the result is disconnection. High-conflict couples are usually bad news because the relationships become environments of perpetual upset and dysregulation. These are the couples that *need* therapy. If this is you, *run* (do not walk) to therapy. No one wants to be in a constant state of disagreement.

Mark and Bianca entered therapy through conflict. Even during their first sessions, their arguing gave me a headache, and I told them as much. One day, each was going on and on about how they felt the other one wasn't listening to them. Round and round they went, each ignoring the other, each demanding accountability for the exact same thing.

> BIANCA: It's like you don't care. I ask for one simple thing, and you say you're going to do it and never follow through. Tell me how I am supposed to respond.
>
> MARK: Factually, that is not what happened. You asked me to make dinner reservations by saying, "You forgot to make reservations, again." And that pissed me off, and I didn't want to do anything at that point.
>
> BIANCA: Yeah, it's because you never listen to me! It's like everything I say just goes in one ear and out the other!
>
> MARK: I'm listening! I just don't agree, that's all! Objectively, this just isn't what happened. I feel like I'm walking on eggshells with you *all the time*. Nothing is ever good enough.
>
> BIANCA: I just can't with you, when you get defensive like

this. Anytime I point something out, you freak out and fight me on it. Making dinner reservations isn't rocket science.

ME: Okay, let's pause for a moment. I can see that both of you are feeling very frustrated right now. This cycle of argument that you're stuck in, it's exhausting, isn't it? I'm finding it tough to keep up, too. It's giving me a headache, and I'm not even part of this relationship. No wonder you two are so miserable. *This* is misery. Let's take a step back.

MARK: We're not trying to give you a headache, but . . .

I interrupted. (I interrupt a lot.)

ME: I know you're not, Mark. And that's my point. This isn't working for any of us.

In many relationships, when a disagreement arises, we can respond in ways that make it worse. And we keep using the same ineffective method only to then exclaim, "I don't know what to do! I've tried everything." Mark and Bianca coped with their disappointment and managed conflict by using the very same method they had as children.

Any expression of disappointment was experienced as criticism or rejection. And any withdrawal felt like abandonment. Both stances of their present dynamic were rooted in their childhoods, and I spent a significant amount of time hammering this point home for them. (Much of my work as a therapist, in fact, requires a lot of convincing.) Both Mark and Bianca had had abandoning and critical parents, and their early wounds were being triggered.

The task at hand for Mark was to hear his partner's expressions of disappointment without personalizing or internalizing them to the point where he was consumed and defined by them (just as he had been by his mother's criticisms). The task at hand for Bianca was to see Mark's withdrawal without feeling abandoned (just as she had in the face of her mother and father's withdrawal).

It was tough work. Why? Because Bianca's requests *were* critical, and Mark's response of withdrawing or shutting down *did* resemble abandonment. Their responses to each other unintentionally magnified the very behaviors they wished to diminish. Bianca felt abandoned, and when she criticized Mark, she inadvertently encouraged his distancing behavior. Conversely, Mark felt criticized, yet by withdrawing and shutting down, he inadvertently invited more criticism; his actions almost guaranteed that Bianca would feel displeased and disappointed.

But the intensity of each one's reaction to the other's withdrawal or criticism wasn't rooted in their current relationship but, instead, stemmed from the deep-seated pain of similar criticisms, rejections, and abandonments they had experienced in childhood.

This is where differentiation comes in. The differentiated person says, "I understand that you're upset with me, but your perception of me doesn't define who I am. Therefore, I am more capable of listening to your thoughts and feelings with respect and without needing to defend myself because I'm not defined by your point of view." This creates space for curiosity, which can help partners express empathy and understanding.

So, my primary approach with Mark and Bianca involved helping them connect better with themselves first, particularly when receiving feedback from each other. For example, when Bianca criticized Mark, Mark learned to say to himself,

I know who I am. I didn't do anything wrong. Bianca is in a bad mood or being triggered. I don't need to become defensive. Her emotions are hers, and I don't need to take responsibility for them. Each had to show up for themselves and prioritize their own emotional well-being, an experience they had never been given throughout childhood.

For many of us, no one showed up for us when we were little, which makes it hard for us to show up for ourselves as adults. Instead, we want our partner to show up for us, even during conflict and disagreement. Unfortunately, adult partnership doesn't work like this.

Mark and Bianca both had wounds, and we spent a considerable amount of time in session exploring them. The truth is, some wounds will never completely heal. We soften those wounds by shifting our current perspective and making changes in our relationships that decrease the frequency and intensity of wounding. If you want to call that a resolution, go for it. I wouldn't, because at some point the past will come up again. (And for Mark and Bianca, it did.)

Navigating perpetual challenges can be complex for both therapists and clients. When issues surface, we often crave solutions. Yet there are times when the answer isn't clear-cut. Instead, it may be more about embracing acceptance, practicing tolerance, or offering forgiveness.

Mark and Bianca had never managed to confront or truly understand their parents, let alone reach a point where forgiveness could enter those past relationships. Yet this ability to understand became a pivotal step in their adult relationship with each other, particularly given that both wrestled with similar themes.

In session, we focused on their accepting the parts of their relationship that seemed resistant to change, particularly their impressive talent for triggering each other, much as their parents had done. I guided them toward adopting a mindset of acceptance, of learning to embrace the imperfections and constraints inherent in their dynamic.

Mark and Bianca were perplexed by my intervention. There were still parts of them that craved a solution. So, I asked them, "Why stay together?" This is a fun and daring question. Some couples pause, slow to start listing their reasons. They say things like "We have kids" or "I love him." But kids and love aren't enough.

However, when I asked them, Mark quickly said, "Oh, I love Bianca. Her attitude, the way she expresses her love, and I deeply admire her work and intellectual passions."

Bianca quickly said, "I just think Mark is a genius, and I have fun sharing a life with him."

Then I asked, "Do you enjoy being with each other?"

They both said yes.

The point is that they thoroughly enjoyed each other, but there were times when conflict arose and they became so preoccupied and anxious over it (triggered) that they would enter gridlock—unable to let it go or resolve it. It was when they resisted entering a particular conflict that they were able to connect with the positive feelings they had about each other. I helped them accept that this part of their relationship didn't have to be scary, as it was when they were younger; that a rupture could be followed by a repair that would make conflict feel less like a death sentence. I encouraged them to play with this approach, or maybe even to learn to laugh at their conflicts. Humor is important.

It was an imperfect relationship, but for them, it was good enough.

HUMOR

I make a conscious effort to bring humor into my conversations; I try to make my clients laugh at least once per session. I firmly believe that humor can help repair in the process of healing. Remember the saying "Laughter is the best medicine?" The ability to laugh at our own shortcomings and errors allows us to create a cushion around otherwise painful realities. Life's inherent absurdities and the often bewildering complexities of relationships require that we embrace laughter even more. Humor plays a critical role not just in therapy but also in relationships, love, and even during intimate moments. It has the power to transform fear and anxiety into joy and connectivity, to lighten the heavy load we carry. And it provides a stark contrast to many of our childhood experiences, where normal disappointments or conflicts might have escalated into calamities. By inviting laughter into these spaces, we soften the edges of past trauma and disappointments, allowing ourselves to navigate life's complexities with a lighter heart and a more resilient spirit. So, laugh more.

BUT WHAT ABOUT COMMUNICATION?

Instead of having Mark and Bianca learn about differentiation, many therapists would have had them complete communication exercises where they held space for each other and validated each other's experiences.

Yes, communication is important. We hear about it until we're all blue in the face:

Use "I" statements.

Repeat what your partner has said.

Hold space.

Honor their emotions. Yes, do a little validation. "I can see how you might feel that way."

Stay calm. If possible. And if not, take a break.

(All these should be kind of obvious.)

While this may sound sweet and nice, the reality of relationships is far from that simple. Of course it's important to communicate kindly, to validate your partner, and to hold space for their feelings (yes, please be nice!), but these alone won't be enough to achieve fulfillment in a relationship. Not to mention that when our trauma is triggered all bets are off.

Sure, we all want solutions, and it's definitely easier to think the solution to your problem requires a simple logistical adjustment involving different words rather than a complete restructuring of your entire relational dynamic and psyche. And yes, sometimes new words, a softer tone, or even a hand on your partner's thigh accompanied by eye contact can and do make a difference. But the truth is, relationships are complex and require much more than just good communication skills.

If you're just looking to feel good in the moment when you communicate with your partner, then you're not seeking real, honest communication. You're not seeking intimacy. You're looking for comfort and acceptance, which are totally different things from honesty and intimacy. Schnarch says, "We're driven by something that makes us look like we crave intimacy, but in fact we're after something else; we want someone else to make us feel acceptable and worthwhile. We've assigned the label 'intimacy' to what we want (validation and reciprocal disclosure) and developed pop psychologies that give it to us— while keeping true intimacy away."

True intimacy requires a willingness to be uncomfortable, to hear what you don't want to hear. With that in mind, I'm going to ask you to let go of some big things here.

Let go of the expectation that your partner (or anyone, for that matter) should validate, accept, take care of, or hold space for your emotions before theirs; should agree with you all the time; or should be your savior. It may feel like you *need* this, but you don't. We have to learn how to feel comfortable and confident in our own skin first, before demanding that our partners do so for us.

Let go of the idea that your feelings are true or need to be validated in the first place. They are not valid or invalid. They just *are*. The rain is rain. The sky is the sky. We don't question them; we simply observe them. That is the relationship you want to cultivate with your emotions—especially when triggered and especially when in conflict. Connect to the past and present experiences your emotions are pointing to. This is the power of storytelling. A story is neither valid nor invalid. It just is; it is experience with details.

Don't think for a second that I'm encouraging you to enter

unhappy or abusive relationships. I am instead encouraging you to fundamentally change how you understand yourself in the context of relationships.

LOVE AND HATE ARE TWO SIDES OF THE SAME COIN

There are going to be things that drive you absolutely bananas about your partner and everyone else on this planet. You may even feel you hate them at times. This is normal and not a problem . . . unless you start to define your partner only by the traits driving you crazy.

The challenge is to allow yourself to feel frustrated, disappointed, hateful, even, without assigning that feeling to your relationship or your partner. You can do so by reminding yourself of everything your partner does have to offer (assuming they offer you something).

The one simple fact you need to accept is that the satisfaction of our relationships does not, cannot, depend on whether your partner has certain characteristics. They are definitionally flawed, as are we. But it is how we understand and deal with those flaws that affects how happy we are in our relationships.

If you want to engage in intimacy as an adult, you must understand your partner's flaws based on their personal history and not the implications of their flaws for your fulfillment. This is called empathy. Alain de Botton used the expression "loveable idiot" for this perspective on your partner, which I love. We can be in relationships with people who will make us lose our minds and still love and respect them.

This is a message we almost never receive. We are told to

be independent, to defend ourselves, not to let anyone ever hurt us, and if they do, to leave them because they are moth-erfucking toxic.

It's time for a rewrite. Try the following narrative on for size. See how it fits. Consider whether it stirs anything up:

I can impact my relationships by changing myself.
I don't need to wait for someone else to change.
I don't need permission to have certain needs or
    preferences.
I am not clairvoyant and don't know what change exists in
    the future.
I can stop questioning whether the relationship can
    change.
Instead, I will push myself to be the one to change.
I will become aware of my triggers, conscious of how
    my past shapes my present, and work on doing things
    differently.

No one can replace the relationship you have with your-self. No one can come first. *You* must come first for *yourself.* Don't confuse this with a lack of regard for your partner. This is about making yourself a priority in all the relational contexts in which you seek connection.

The way we make ourselves a priority is by understanding the role we play in both our fulfilling and unfulfilling dynamics. If you want to shift your focus, you cannot do so by engaging in constant surveillance of your partner. You must accept that love and hate, love and fear, love and "I lose my mind when you leave all the kitchen cabinet doors open" are all realities that will shape your relationship. The way we respond in these situations, as well as the dynamics that lead up to them, have a big impact on how others will react.

We impact our partner just as much as they impact us; we elicit reactions and behaviors from others. This is the cycle of action-reaction that influences the ebb and flow of connection in our relationships. We ask a question, and we get a response. Each interaction prompts a counteraction, subtly influencing the rhythm of our relationship. If we're feeling upset from the night prior and communicate in a nasty or overly critical tone of voice, it's likely our partner will respond similarly or retreat. It doesn't matter if our resentment is appropriate. If we allow that resentment to color our subsequent interactions, our partner will pick up on it, even if we're dead silent. Sometimes it's the silence that is the worst.

The more curiosity, accountability, compassion, and kindness we bring into a dynamic, the more we increase the likelihood of collaboration and connection. Even when we feel we're the one who has been wronged or it's a hopeless case.

This is what I deeply struggled to understand, accept, and change within myself.

Alex and I were anything but differentiated. We were co-dependent, and both of us became gradually resentful of the lack of independence our relationship afforded us. My differentiation from the relationship would have required me to use my voice, a lot, to push Alex, but not to change him, to share what I wanted and why. I wanted to have deeper conversations about our conflicts and to actively work on our relationship. Whether in reading self-help books, taking courses, or entering therapy, I could have allowed him to see this part of myself rather than merely hoping he would initiate the discussion. I could have made an appointment for us to go to couples therapy, even if he didn't want to. I could have bought self-help books and said, "Okay, it's reading time! Let's sit and read out loud to each other." I was the therapist, after all! It was totally within my wheelhouse to spearhead such a project.

But I needed to understand that his resistance was about his own issues and that I didn't have to be defined by them. I could have spoken up when I wanted something different, and then respected and tolerated him when he couldn't provide it. Sometimes, we don't necessarily need the change we believe we do; sometimes, we simply want connection and acknowledgment.

NO ONE WANTS A SECOND CHILDHOOD

Childhood is choiceless. As a kid, I didn't have a choice, and neither did you. No child does. Alain de Botton humorously yet accurately writes, "Even when things are going right, childhood is a gentle open prison." We kids couldn't just go to the store and get another family. We all had to settle with the family we had. Even if that required us to normalize abuse or become powerless.

The one good thing my parents did for me was put me in therapy at a young age. And I was lucky enough eventually to find someone to stand in as a surrogate parent, my therapist Derek. He was the only one who validated my emotions, who made me feel safe as a child.

A lack of choice is what I swore to myself I would not re-create as an adult. I would choose where I lived, whom I spent my time with, and quite literally everything. But it took me a very long time to get to the point where my adulthood didn't look or feel like my childhood. And I'm still working on it. I still isolate and hide. I still speak quietly. I'm a work in progress. We all are.

I learned that you can't undo the traumas of childhood by doing in adulthood what was done back then. I was doing that with Alex. As were my clients. And you might be, too. I withdrew during difficult times in my relationships and, as a result, felt as alone and abandoned as I had as a child. This was my second childhood. Psychiatrist Thomas Szasz writes, "Every act of conscious learning requires the willingness to suffer an injury to one's self-esteem." Unfortunately, with Alex, I was in a defended state and unable to confront my inner demons because my unconscious was doing its best to stop me from confronting the painful losses of my childhood, leaving me oblivious to what was actually going on in our dynamic and inside my mind. We can change only when we face the stories we've told ourselves about who we are, who our partner is, and what we feel we need in order to be satisfied. Psycho-therapist Lori Gottlieb writes, "We can't have change without loss, which is why so often people say they want change but nonetheless stay exactly the same." In essence, the resistance to change is a resistance to loss. And this was the story that prevented me from acting on behalf with Alex and changing myself.

Earlier, I talked about how we can re-enact patterns and dynamics from childhood in our adult life, which is similar to what I'm referring to as a second childhood. This is when our childhood experiences completely shape our adult relationships. With wise insight, Carl Jung noted, "Until you make the unconscious conscious, it will direct your life and you will call it fate." While we all re-create aspects of our childhood in adulthood, some people do so more than others. We do this until, one day, we reach a breaking point or enter a crisis and are forced to pause and reflect. Psychologist Tara Brach writes, "Perhaps the biggest tragedy of our lives is that freedom is possible, yet we can pass our years trapped in the same old patterns." These patterns continue to have a hold over us all until we find the courage to confront the realities of our lives and break free from the familiar yet restrictive patterns we've become accustomed to.

We accomplish this by investing in our own capacity to drive change in our lives and positively influence our relationships, even if our partner isn't matching our effort.

What happens when only one person in a relationship does the work? Change still happens! Why? Because when we change, our relationship changes.

Maybe you worry you'll resent your partner if they don't match your effort to change. Ask yourself this: Why? If we can change our relationships for the better by doing work on ourselves alone, why resent our partner for not doing the same amount of work? Well, because we often expect a relationship to be a fifty-fifty proposition. I'm sorry, but once again, you're going to have to let go of this.

The fundamental idea here is that we don't need to rely on our partners to be the ones initiating change. Waiting for them to take the lead can often lead to a re-enactment of the powerlessness we experienced in childhood. Instead, we can actively transform our relationships by first making changes within ourselves.

This is what it means to differentiate.

This is what it means to grow up.

8

Too Good to Leave, Too Bad to Stay

Lovers pass constantly from rapture to despair, from sadness to joy, from wrath to tenderness, from desperation to sensuality. . . . The lover is perpetually driven by contradictory emotions.

—OCTAVIO PAZ

A HARD PILL TO SWALLOW

Relationships are often seen as a binary portrayal of health. We are presented with polarizing and oversimplified choices: good or bad, red flag or green flag, leave or stay.

My clients often pose questions like:

"Are they the wrong partner for me?"

"Should I continue dating this person?"

"Is it a red flag? Are they toxic???"

In our quest for self-improvement, we often crave absolutism and certainty. Some people go on one date, use the limited data they've gathered to make assumptions about their potential future, and quickly decide whether or not it could work. Similarly, people in relationships may encounter challenges or differences and quickly end things. But is this approach the right one? Can we be too impulsive? The truth is, there isn't a definitive answer.

The end of a relationship can be just as uncertain as its beginning.

In my relationship with Alex, I wanted answers and desperately sought them from my therapist and friends. My friends recommended creating lists of pros and cons, but I soon realized that this approach falls short when it comes to relationships. The classification of something as a "pro" or a "con" can fluctuate depending on the day or even the hour. When Alex and I had fun together or a night of hot sex, it was easier to overlook his limitations and connect with the desire to stay in the relationship forever. However, at other times, when those moments were absent, our relationship felt downright terrible.

Relationships are anything but black and white; they consistently defy the objective understanding often presented on social media. Sure, make the pro/con list, but don't pressure yourself to think that once you have it will bring you new insights. Sometimes these lists provide clarity, but more often they only exacerbate the existing panic and uncertainty. I still made the list. And while it was helpful to get my regular spirals down on paper, it did nothing to help me understand how to move forward.

My friends wanted me to leave Alex because I only ever seemed to complain about him when I was with them. My family loved Alex and didn't understand why I'd ever consider leaving. And my therapist, Derek, helped me understand the nuance and complexity of the situation. Derek could have pushed me to leave, but instead, he helped me use the experience to learn more about myself.

The decision weighed heavily on me, leaving me paralyzed and adrift for almost two years. My paralysis stemmed largely from the idea that I ought to have an unwavering certainty about what I wanted. But the reality was that my relationship with Alex was a complex and nuanced paradox, a confusing dance between enjoying the bond we shared and yearning for something more.

The prevailing advice in our culture encourages us to end relationships that are not wholly fulfilling, to steer clear from people who are what we've now come to label as "unavailable," to hyper-analyze each red flag and look for green flags, and to create mental Excel spreadsheets to determine if our partner is wrong for us. The detective work we do is out of control.

In addressing infidelity, Esther Perel observes that "the new shame is staying." However, this sentiment goes beyond just infidelity; it encompasses any relationship that doesn't meet our expectations for complete fulfillment or fails to align with the societal ideals we're encouraged to pursue. The shame we experience arises not only from remaining in imperfect relationships but also from silently settling for less than what we truly desire and have been led to believe (often by strangers on the internet) that we deserve. In fact, the online therapy space is littered with checklists that aim to identify "bad" partners, accompanied by theories attempting to shed light on why people are drawn to or can't break away from such people.

I am neither advocating for nor discouraging anyone from staying in unfulfilling relationships or dating someone who is incapable of giving them what they seek. Instead, I want you to think deeper about what keeps us connected. The truth is, whether a relationship is in its early stages or has spanned two decades of marriage, encountering challenges or red flags is quite normal, and navigating a path forward can be a complex, triggering task.

EMMA OWNS HER POWER

Emma, a forty-four-year-old heterosexual cisgender white woman, initially sought therapy for her chronic anxiety—which was unsurprising, given a history of childhood trauma that included sexual assault, neglect, and abandonment. Emma also struggled with bulimia and body dysmorphic disorder. During therapy sessions, it became apparent that she had grown up in a family where she was the scapegoat, considered the "bad object." Her family gave her derogatory nicknames and neglected her, which made Emma feel she was "too much" for wanting basic comfort, love, and affection.

When telling me about the name-calling, Emma did so with a laugh and a seemingly unbothered expression. This happens with many clients. They often present something terrible, abusive, or heartbreaking from an unemotional place. This is because they've never been allowed to and/or haven't let themselves confront the reality implied by these loss-oriented experiences. When this happens, I will react as if it were me, to model to them that it is okay to feel, to react, and to be upset.

When Emma told me about her family's hurtful nicknames for her, I said, "What the actual fuck? That is terrible, Emma. These names are not terms of endearment. What did you say when they called you this?"

She said, "I would say nothing and laugh it off."

"Well, say something!" I exclaimed. "Be direct, and say plainly, 'I do not like when you call me this name. Stop, and don't do it again.'"

This was just the tip of the iceberg. Both of Emma's parents also had eating disorders and abused alcohol. This led to Emma's development of an eating disorder and a significant anxiety disorder, both of which became ways for her to control her environment and cope with her unmet needs and feelings of powerlessness. Emma's anxiety was something she came to rely on; it became a part of her identity, as it kept her safe. However, as an adult, she was having all the same symptoms of her earlier childhood trauma (e.g., anxiety, panic, paranoia, and a deep conviction that the world disliked her). While Emma was fully aware of her earlier trauma and the potential for its impacting the present, the emotional dysregulation she experienced was so powerful that she was not able to fully integrate new insights during times of upheaval. The result? She re-enacted the same dynamics of powerlessness with her partner that she had experienced with her parents.

While her partner was definitionally unlike her parents— he was kind, attentive, and practically too willing to be her caretaker—he was also cheating on her. The discovery of his infidelity cut Emma deep and caused her to remain in a constant state of hypervigilance. She clung to the hope that her partner could rescue her from her anxiety and provide a sense of security to repair the trust he had broken.

Emma made the choice to try to salvage her marriage. She and her husband had a decade-long history together, and she wanted to give their future a shot. I supported her decision, given that her partner, based on her reports of him, was otherwise caring and sincere. We even held a few couples therapy sessions during which he expressed remorse and a deep desire to make amends.

However, the journey was strenuous for Emma. Trust, once shattered, is challenging to restore for anyone with chronic anxiety and a history of trauma. It can be said that powerful feelings in the present reflect a deep connection to the past. However, that is not to discount the relevance they have in our present, too. I knew something was off.

Then, a year later, another particular incident opened the floodgates and led to the revelation that he had been unfaithful several times throughout their relationship and marriage from the very beginning. This left Emma heartbroken, her trust in him destroyed.

In therapy, a lot of focus is placed on past wounds and traumas. But if we're to be adults and have satisfying lives, we must, to some extent, leave the past behind. If we spend too much time unpacking, reprocessing, and trying to "resolve" early traumas, nothing in the present changes. Change happens in the *doing*. Change happens when we use the information learned from our past to modify our behavior in the *present*.

At times, this change involves staying and actively working

on our relationship, while in other instances, it requires us to make the difficult choice to leave. For Emma, it became clear that it was time to let go. Her relationship mirrored the dysfunctional dynamics she had endured in her past. Her chronic anxiety didn't stem from a chemical imbalance or genetics; rather, it was a profound indicator of just how unsafe and unreliable relationships had been in her life. And her partner was no different.

The biggest challenge for Emma was investing in her own power, the power that was taken from her during childhood. Emma and I discussed how by choosing an adult life defined by the same powerlessness she had experienced as a girl—powerlessness over her relationships, her body, and the world—she remained unconsciously loyal to her family. In every session, we talked about power—and it became clear that she was afraid of her power. She was afraid to grow up. She had identified with her wounds. By silencing herself and denying herself agency in adulthood, she was still trying to be a good daughter. She would often say things like "I can't handle this," "It's going to destroy me," "He broke me," and "He ruined our life." She was still in the space of victimization and woundedness she had occupied throughout her childhood and adolescence. Her words were not about her present reality; they were about her past.

I said to Emma what Derek had said to me: "Those are the words you would have used if you had been able to."

As we grow up, we develop the vocabulary, the insight, and the ability to confront and ask for things at a time, adulthood, when we actually no longer need them. For Emma, her expressions of "I can't handle this" and "It's going to destroy me" were not solely about her current adult relationship. They were reflections on the deep pain she had experienced during her childhood, which felt unbearable and beyond her capacity to cope with. Her current pain, although profound and intense, was something she could manage. After all, she was no longer a helpless child dependent on unhealthy caregivers. She was an empowered, insightful, intelligent, and successful adult fully competent in caring for herself without anyone's assistance.

In focusing on the process of grieving her irretrievable losses, Emma gradually began to move forward with a divorce, recognizing the need to occupy a powerful position as the competent adult she had become. By exploring the connection between her present emotions and the unresolved pain from her past, Emma was able to gain insight into the narratives that had influenced her current experiences and finally claim her power.

Being able to choose who we are, how we act, and what we do in response to unmet needs or an unsatisfying life is a superpower. In order to tap into this power, this choice, we must develop the understanding that, unlike in childhood with our family of origin, as adults we can have a positive impact on our relationships.

This is how we heal in the context of our adult relationships. As adults, we are finally able to push for more and to negotiate our needs. But the only way we can do so is through self-empowerment, partnership, and teamwork—not entitlement or objectification. The road to healing isn't always straightforward. Sometimes, it involves staying and working through the tough spots. At other times, it requires the courage to leave. Both choices can bring healing.

Ultimately, my solution was to leave.

ALEX AND ME: A QUESTION OF TRUST

I disliked living in Florida and had never wanted to stay there permanently. After about seven-ish years, I was going stir crazy. I wanted to be back in New York City, the place where I felt the safest and most inspired.

Alex knew I wanted to leave Florida, but he had made his stance clear: He was never leaving. A direct quote: "I am never leaving." He was making the most money he had ever made and was convinced that leaving his job would spell the end of his financial success. Starting over wasn't something he was willing to do. I tried to persuade him that a move to New York City would open up new opportunities for salary growth, but he wasn't interested. So, after one discussion, I took his response as a firm "no."

I couldn't simply accept that and stay in Florida. So, I told him that I would move north without him. And I did.

I had never thought I would have a long-distance relationship, but it wasn't as bad as I'd anticipated. It reinvigorated our relationship and I actually liked it. If you want to be in a long-distance relationship, you can make it work. But you'll have to have your virtual relationship skills down pat. And Alex and I were actually pretty damn good at it. We FaceTimed daily, texted constantly, had virtual sex all the time, sexted, and did everything we could to keep our love and life together alive. We even had date nights, watching the same movie together while on FaceTime. It was very cute.

I would travel back and forth between New York City and Florida pretty regularly; I can't believe it now, but I made the trip about every other week. Alex didn't come to New York, though. I never pushed because I assumed that it would be best for our dog, Zoey, who had stayed with Alex in Florida. I wonder now if his opposition to coming to New York was the way he unconsciously communicated and punished me for leaving him. But of course, this can only be an assumption, because I never actually asked him.

Alex and I stayed monogamous . . . until I wanted to see other people. I cringe when I look back on this, because I was extremely selfish. I basically gave him an ultimatum: I told him I would leave if the relationship couldn't be an open one. This was very off-brand for me, as I don't believe that handing down ultimatums is ever an effective way to negotiate. Ultimatums are also unhealthy, and I wasn't even someone who enjoyed casual sex! But after having spent all of my twenties with Alex, a sense of curiosity and an interest in something new had stirred within me. I was definitely not ready to sever our bond, but I felt the need for exploration. In retrospect, I now know this was an unconscious attempt to end the relationship. I was, to say the least, quite confused.

Eventually Alex caved, and we experimented for two months. But I was quickly reminded of how little I enjoyed sex with strangers and of how much I enjoyed sex and felt most comfortable with Alex. Strangers always smell odd to me, and I am sensitive to odd smells. They make weird, unfamiliar noises, and I am sensitive to weird noises. It's one thing if your partner makes a weird noise during sex, because you know them well and their noises are made within the context of an entire spectrum of noises that are familiar and, therefore, normal for you. But it's quite another thing when a stranger does it, at least for me. They *become* the weird noise. I just couldn't do it.

So, we decided to close the relationship back up again—or so I thought.

One weekend, I was in Florida with him as he prepared to leave for a conference. I had accompanied him to the same conference the previous year, and I remembered its being one big party—lots of drugs, alcohol, clubs. So, I was nervous about his going. I was always anxious that he would cheat on me, and I think part of me knew it would happen one day.

And it did.

During that visit before his trip, we had a wonderful time, and a lot of hot sex. We talked about our future, children, and more. Things felt great . . . until I noticed that he had been manscaping, taking a little too much care with his body hair when no one else was supposed to be seeing it. I asked him why he was bothering to shave his balls and his taint before a trip *without* his boyfriend, and he said the hair there made him feel dirty. LIES. I didn't believe him. The truth was so obvious. Whether or not Alex was consciously aware of it, his freshly shaved balls knew the plan. Again, I didn't push.

I flew back to New York, and he went to his conference. I checked in with him regularly by FaceTime; he was acting weird. So, I did what any jealous partner does: I asked him if he was cheating on me. He denied it and said I was crazy. This only escalated my fears.

So, what did I, a rational and insightful person, do? I made a fake profile on Grindr, with a phony location, placing my location at his hotel, and that's when I found him, right there on Grindr! I lost my fucking mind. Truly. I did things I'm sure you would judge me for. I definitely judge myself for them. But at that moment, I had lost sight of everything,

LOVE WILL MAKE YOU LOSE YOUR MIND

Let's be honest—love can make us act out of character, lead us down a path of behavior we might not be proud of. We've all heard it said that love makes us do crazy things, and it's true. That's not to say we should embrace or excuse such actions. Quite the contrary: We should always avoid decisions in the present that lead to later regret. But let's acknowledge that sometimes we falter. We all have moments that don't showcase us at our finest, and this was one of mine. And, boy, did I falter!

One part love mixed with two parts insecurity and suspicion can blur our judgment. We can become so triggered that we act out. It's important, especially when navigating the madness of dating, to exercise self-control, respect boundaries, and communicate openly. That is, if you can. Remember, we're all human, and we all make mistakes, but it's through those mistakes that we learn and grow.

Furious, I messaged him as the fake person. I asked him about what he had been up to. And I asked if he had hooked up with anyone. The answer: He had.

Then I immediately called and texted him as myself and asked him if he had hooked up. There I was, talking to him through my fake Grindr profile while he was assuring the real me that he wasn't hooking up with anyone. Meanwhile, he was making plans to hook up with some random stranger me!

I was *enraged*. But instead of telling him his potential Grindr hookup was actually me, I kept the ruse going. I didn't let on that it was me until days later. I waited for him to come clean, but instead, he gaslit me: "You are crazy and need to stop."

This was the moment our relationship fell apart. It wasn't so much because he had fucked some other guy and who knew what else. I of course was enraged about that, but his lying was the betrayal that broke me; it seemed to reflect that he didn't have the maturity or self-awareness to communicate what had happened and why. He had always struggled to express his emotions, and instead of trying now, he denied both his own feelings and mine.

Alex wasn't a bad person. He didn't even know what he was doing or how he was communicating. It was all instinct and impulse. And he made an incredibly stupid and hurtful decision by lying to me and then denying it, even when caught red-handed.

Eventually we did some work to figure out what had happened. I learned a lot about myself, our relationship, love, and trust. Alex's heart had been broken when I went to New York without him, but he had never verbalized this to me. The night we decided to transition to a long-distance relationship, he had gotten so drunk that he fainted. But he never used any *words* to communicate to me what his acting out implied. Still, while he didn't express it, he was feeling abandoned. He felt that by moving to New York, I was essentially breaking up with him. Which, on some level, I was.

Ultimately, I can't know exactly what he was feeling. I believe that he, like many people who can't communicate their emotions, enacts their emotions behaviorally. He did so by cheating, withholding information, blaming and gaslighting me. I think what he was trying to say was, *I want to feel valued. I feel like you keep leaving me. It makes me feel tossed aside. Where do I stand? Where do we stand?* But he never said this. And I never asked.

Instead, he cheated, and I lost my mind.

Alex eventually took responsibility and apologized to me. Begged and pleaded, in fact. Did the whole dance of remorse. But his remorse lasted only until he grasped the idea that his cheating had been a response to our upsetting relational dynamics. Looking back on this chapter, I see that we didn't do the best job at managing it. We went to a terrible couples therapist who made us practice communication exercises but never actually did anything for us. So, we stopped therapy. We should have gone to another therapist, but I convinced myself that it was a waste of time. Big mistake. We had a few sessions with Derek, but that was it.

Regardless of whether you're contemplating breaking up, seeking counseling should be your first line of defense. In the worst-case scenario, you might still choose to part ways, but you'll have a professional on hand to guide you through it. On the brighter side, you may learn new methods of managing disagreements, which can lead to the formation of a stronger, healthier bond.

The limits of Alex's remorse weren't about a lack of empathy. Instead, this reflected the limits of his ability to process and communicate his emotions. He never described what was actually happening to him. Derek put it into words, and Alex agreed, but that was kind of it. Ideally, gaining clearer insight into his motivations would have led to the realization that more understanding and change were required.

Alex should have seen his own therapist, to learn what shut him down so much, not only from me but from himself. Why wasn't he sharing his pain with me? Why was he sharing it with me by hurting me? What were the origins of this? I pushed the idea of solo therapy, but he didn't want to go, and I was sick of having to be the one to tell him to do it.

What surprised me most was how hot I found his cheating. Obviously, it was painful but once I moved past the shock (sort of), it became the biggest turn-on. I wanted him to tell me about it. I fantasized about it. We started having threesomes. It reinvigorated our sex life. It's not that we needed any reinvigoration; we were always on fire in bed. But it was as if the cheating had poured gasoline on that fire. It was hard for us to keep our hands off each other. On one level, it helped bring us back together. As Esther Perel writes, there is an "intense erotic charge that sometimes follows the discovery of an affair." And there definitely was quite a charge for us.

But I never trusted him again.

Then, three years later, we went on a cruise with his family. At dinner one night, we discussed with his parents the prospect of having children. It felt nice and exciting. Later, I couldn't find Alex for about an hour . . . until I saw him walking out of a bathroom off the ship's deck with a young guy (twink).

I lost my mind—again. Like totally lost my shit and transformed into a completely different person.

During that night on the cruise, everything broke. Alex denied having cheated, but his actions weren't innocent. That moment marked the beginning of the end. It wasn't about the truth versus a lie or his having done who knew what with some random guy. It was about my realization that it didn't matter what had happened because I didn't believe anything he had to say; the truth was irrelevant as there was no remaining trust to be found.

I am generally able to keep my composure, especially in public. I don't believe in fighting or having conflict in front of others, particularly family members. And a family vacation aboard a ship is neither the time nor the place. Keeping my composure in public is not about privacy or appropriateness, but about productivity. Genuine, transparent, and vulnerable discussions cannot unfold in the presence of an audience.

I stopped speaking to him. It was the maddest I had ever been at him. We returned home, and I was set to go back to New York.

I was colder than ice. It was over. 😥

Infidelity is awful. It can stir up the wildest emotions and behaviors. From snooping to revenge fucks—most people lose their minds. First, that's okay. It's okay to feel big things, to do "crazy" things. It's fine. If you want to work through infidelity, you can. Many couples I see who have experienced infidelity do, in fact, recover and go on to form a new relationship that is stronger and more connected (sexually and nonsexually) than before. In some cases, infidelity can be the catalyst for healing, a painful catalyst, but one that nonetheless can bring about positive results. Yet just as many couples do not recover from infidelity and end decade-long relationships. It just goes to show you how deep betrayal can cut.

There is a certain threshold beyond which we will not allow our partner to pass, and for many, that line is infidelity. For some, cheating is a moral issue, with the cheater often stigmatized with a scarlet letter. The belief that "once a cheater, always a cheater" prevails, and while some unfaithful partners are also abusive, not all cheaters are inherently bad. Infidelity is not an accident, but a response to a deep-seated longing, whether it be for something missing in the relationship or within oneself. However, it is not an effective way to address any issue. Open and honest conversation and other constructive efforts that don't cause harm to others are a better approach.

Cheating and infidelity are very complicated. It's rare that it's a case of someone who is just being a narcissistic asshole. Don't get me wrong; there are plenty of assholes out there. But the reality is that infidelity arises from a meaningful relational dynamic—not pathology. This isn't to minimize the seismic quake an infidelity can cause to a relationship. But you have to understand that cheating is here to stay. And we would all be better served to work on understanding it rather than immediately condemning it.

You absolutely cannot work through it alone. In the aftermath of an infidelity, the flood of emotions can be so overwhelming that it will diminish each partner's capacity for rational decision-making and clear thinking. (Love really *can* make you crazy in these instances.) Seeking the help of a neutral third party to mediate the recovery process is necessary, even if you're considering ending the relationship. Go to your own personal therapist. Go to couples counseling. Just don't throw in the towel too quickly. Don't take this as a mandate, but rather as something to consider, especially if the relationship held significant value and brought you joy. Remember, it's worth exploring the possibility of healing and growth before making a final decision.

ALEX AND ME: NO ONE'S FAULT

Ultimately, my decision was to end the relationship. Not because I didn't love Alex—I did, more than I had loved anyone in my life—and not because he had cheated, and not because he had lied, although that certainly pushed me over the edge. I ended it because I didn't see a way forward for us. I couldn't trust that when something challenging arose in our relationship again he would be open and honest with me. Maybe it *wasn't* all about the cheating. Maybe it *was* all about the cheating. I don't know. I do know that I didn't hate him for it. I wasn't angry about it. I was just very sad.

I wanted us to remain together. I really did. But I knew that part of me just couldn't. It probably would have been easier for me to blame his cheating, to tell myself, *He cheated, lied, and gaslit you. You need to get away from that level of toxicity.* Many people do this. They blame the other person: "It was *his* fault; *he* did this to me." Anger is often an easier way for us to separate ourselves from a situation than is facing the sadness and grief of loss. But it was no one's fault. Alex and I were simply different. We had grown apart. It hadn't worked out.

Regrettably, it was only after getting distance from the relationship that I started to comprehend my own inability to tolerate certain aspects of it and of Alex. I began to recognize the rigidity of my thought patterns, specifically concerning the needs I wanted fulfilled and my reasons behind those needs.

Our beliefs—the ones we feel are absolute truths—can be more flexible than we know, if we're open to being flexible. Our perspectives of others are inherently biased, but they shape our understanding, which dictates our reactions. Yet our perspective is not the absolute or the whole truth. It's merely a specific, subjective interpretation of the world, and susceptible to errors and distortions.

Taking ownership of our biases can lead to valuable insights. In my case, I came to understand that I could have approached Alex's imperfections, which I had once seen as insurmountable, differently. Once I acknowledged this, I saw that I had the power to reshape my perspective, to bring flexibility where once there was only rigidity.

Our attitudes toward and perceptions of our partner significantly influence the overall feel and course of a relationship. If we stubbornly hold on to rigid views, we risk creating unnecessary conflict and dissatisfaction. By opening ourselves to new perspectives, we can create space for understanding, acceptance, and mutual growth.

Alex tried to get me back . . . by doing just about everything except what I *needed* him to do. If he had signed up for therapy, read a self-help book, or begged to go to couples counseling, we could have stayed together, could have had children. But he didn't, and I didn't tell him what I needed in order for us to remain together. I could have, but I didn't. So, I broke our hearts.

The End-ish

All relationships begin, and end, in separation.

—JAMES HOLLIS

F rom Valentine's Day to weddings, anniversaries, honeymoons, engagement parties, bridal showers, bachelor and bachelorette parties—we are obsessed with celebrating love. But what about when a relationship ends? Isn't there something to mark those moments, too? Why aren't we equally obsessed with heartbreak?

Where are the phone apps to help a couple break up? Where are the divorce parties, mirroring the joy of an engagement party? When a relationship comes to an end, it symbolizes a new beginning, too, a chance to redefine oneself. A breakup is a significant life event (perhaps even more significant than an engagement). Yet cultural norms seem to be completely silent on this matter. Most people don't even talk about their breakup. Instead, we ignore, deny, and grieve in silence.

Shouldn't we also uplift and support people when they choose to exit a relationship, just as we cheer them on when they start one?

The decision to end a relationship often comes after much angst and introspection. It takes courage. We could even say that it's harder to end a relationship than to get into one. A breakup can be an important step toward self-growth and personal happiness. It's about time we also honored the courage to let go when things don't work out.

The truth is that beginnings and endings are merely opposite ends of the same spectrum. A relationship's ending is just as meaningful as its beginning. Beginnings are filled with possibility and hope. Endings can be difficult or sad, but they also bring with them growth, understanding, and a chance for self-reflection.

Every relationship, regardless of its duration or intensity, teaches us something about ourselves, about others, and about the meaning of love and connection. An ending, therefore, is not a failure but, rather, a transformative opportunity for growth. It can provide closure, offer perspective, and allow us to better understand our desires, needs, and patterns. And most important, it can lead to better, more satisfying relationships. Which is—hello—a big deal!

In the same vein, endings can be as diverse as beginnings. Some may be abrupt, while others may be gradual; some may be mutual, while others may be one-sided. Regardless of their nature, they deserve as much attention, respect, and understanding as beginnings.

Ironically, the anxiety about a relationship's ending starts right from the beginning, with all the worries over potential hurt and what-ifs to protect us from future pain. We date with laundry lists of needs that we actually don't really need. We play games about when to text back, about what constitutes too quick or too late a reply. Some people will ghost their date. (If that's you, stop it.) Some people guard their emotions, waiting to reveal their "true" selves. We avoid the hard conversations. We lead people on because we don't want to hurt their feelings. And we do all this in the service of avoiding the pain of an ending, any version of an ending.

Ending a relationship—even one with a personal trainer, therapist, or hairstylist—can bring about considerable discomfort. Sometimes it takes months or even years to fully get over it. And ending a friendship? That can be excruciating, often bringing up intense feelings of shame and sadness. I'm even contemplating ending my relationship with New York City, but I can't seem to let go.

ON RELATIONAL ENDINGS

If you're going through some form of a relational ending, keep this in mind.

Relationship endings are a roller-coaster ride, so it's okay to take your time. Sometimes, the emotions linger for years. (I can personally vouch for this.) At other times, the healing process can be easier. The most important thing to remember during a breakup or any significant loss is to prioritize self-care.

Self-care has had a moment over the past five

years, almost to the point where I've rolled my eyes. But it *is* important, especially during loss. Consider the end to a relationship as you might orthopedic surgery. Think knee or hip replacement.

It begins with pain and discomfort. Sometimes, it can be years before we take steps to pursue surgery. We may start with physical therapy or stretching. But at some point, the pain becomes unbearable, and we have no choice. Then we have the surgery (body trauma) and a brief stay in the hospital, followed by a period of rest and immobility at home. In time, you might start taking tentative steps, walking around slowly. Physical therapy is part of your routine, helping you reclaim your life. However, some days might bring back the familiar pain in your joints. All you can do then is take a deep breath, stretch, rest, and provide your body with whatever it needs to soothe the discomfort. It's a process defined by healing and the occasional resurgence of pain. This requires compassion—yes, that often overused term, but it's critical here.

It's essential to share your pain with someone—be it a therapist, a friend, or a family member (but, ideally, a therapist). The burden can feel overwhelmingly heavy, especially in the beginning, and you'll find unexpected memories catching you off guard. So, having a support system is crucial. Last, be patient with the pace of your healing journey and accept where you are at any given moment.

A ROLLER COASTER

I completely broke. Implosion. Explosion.

A self-inflicted amputation of the most loving and stabilizing force in my life.

It was *intense*. No one prepares you for the experience of a relationship's ending. I was devastated, and Alex was devastated. Then there was a long process of him wanting to get back together, me wanting to get back together once he had moved on, then him, then me, and let's just say it was hard. We both missed what we had had and didn't want to let go.

We spent the next three years talking every day, just as we had when we were together, but as "friends." *Friends!*

Cue the judgment. It's okay. I've heard it all:

"That doesn't sound healthy."
"You're addicted to him."
"You should go no contact. That's the best rule."
"Or, maybe just take a break. Stop talking for a while."
"You say you want a relationship, but you're still talking to
      your ex. Do you think that's why you're still single?"

Ugh! Okay, fine. Maybe it wasn't healthy. Maybe we should have stopped talking—or, at least, not talked as much. Perhaps we could have set a boundary or two. Maybe this was why I was still single. (Although, I still don't think that was why. Dating was a different sort of disaster; more on that later.)

This was far more complicated than a simple, objective decision one way or the other.

Cue thousands of Instagram posts encouraging the no-contact rule and implicitly shaming anyone who continues a relationship with their ex. But the story of relationships and their endings is far too complex for us to apply solution-focused changes aimed at reducing pain. Still, every one of my friends and every therapist on Instagram advises against talking to an ex. No contact, cold turkey, zero—a crazy idea to me.

In my work, I've noticed that more than half of my clients will continue to communicate with their former partner, maintaining some form of connection. Even a friendship. This happens despite the discouraging advice recommending a complete cutoff. But we, as a society, might be better off trying to understand our need to continue a connection with an ex than condemning or strongly advising against it. Maybe it's time we reconsidered our attitude toward post-breakup connections. Instead of dismissing them as unhealthy, we could try to understand the motives behind our choice to stay in touch. After all, each relationship and breakup is unique, and the two (or more) people involved in a ruptured relationship are in the best position to judge what serves their emotional needs and personal growth.

The idea of cutting an ex out of your life completely is also extremely heteronormative. Many queer people (like me) don't have their family of origin to fall back on. Our "families" are therefore sometimes our friends, partners, and ex-partners, the people we form deep connections with. Alex was my family for ten years. So, for me, cutting him out of my life entirely wasn't so simple.

AGAIN, IT'S ALL ABOUT THE CONTEXT

At the time of my breakup with Alex, I had a strained relationship with my family members—to the point where it felt like I had no family (which I now don't). So, the idea of suddenly not speaking to someone who had become my family was ridiculous.

Alex and I texted every single day. We talked often. We didn't see each other, but for all emotional intents and purposes, we remained each other's unofficial life partner. On the one hand, this was nice; on the other, I was enacting a type of intimacy without boundaries. Sometimes, he and I would even go through phases of sexting or sending fuck-vids. (I know, not great.)

For a while, neither of us was dating anyone else, so we could serve as each other's Plan B. At least, that is what our interactions suggested to me. And during those interactions, I defaulted to the same place where I had been when we were together: a place of silence and powerlessness. I didn't talk to Alex about it, and he obviously didn't mention it, either.

His behavior suggested that he still had feelings for me, but he also said things like "We're on separate paths." Then he'd text me a "good night," a "good morning," and maybe a dick pic. Looking back, I cannot believe we never addressed these mixed messages. I cannot believe *I* never addressed them. That's literally my job!

If you're going through a breakup, so long as your ex wasn't abusive, talk to them if you want, but address things as needed. Form a totally new relationship with them after the breakup, one defined by different rules. If you avoided difficult conversations when you were together, don't do so with them now, in your new, refashioned relationship. Be honest with yourself, and be brave. If you have residual feelings for your ex, it's okay to remain in contact with them, but make sure to set firm boundaries. Have a conversation with them (and yourself) about what is unfolding. Don't ignore it, even if your ex wants to.

Don't talk to your ex as if they were still your boyfriend/ girlfriend/partner. You don't need to say "I love you" before you take off on a plane if you've broken up. But if you want to stay friends, checking in with them from time to time or just hanging out, I say go ahead. Share professional updates. Share big-deal events and personal milestones.

But I continued to speak to Alex as I had when we were together, and I think this is what kept me stuck. It's maybe even why I remain single to this day. (Perhaps things will be different by the time this book is published. At least, they had better be, or I will be doing my book tour from the inpatient ward at Bellevue.) Professionally, things had started taking off for me, but my personal and family life were going downhill.

For one thing, my father died. He was sick my entire life, and he spent his last living hours with me—just me. And I chose that. Hospice was agony. I remember the odors, the noises. He was a vegetable by this point. I held his hand, and we had *never* held hands. I played his songs—Frank Sinatra's "My Way" and Bob Marley's "Buffalo Soldier"—and I loved him the way I had wanted to be loved by him. I kissed him on the forehead and hugged him. We had never kissed or hugged. I said goodbye. He died an hour after I left.

Alex was there every step along the way (again, we were still broken up). He was there when we got the news with my whole family, and he stayed through shiva and everything else.

We kissed in the driveway that night. I begged him to stay but he didn't. And as per our usual dynamic, we never addressed it. I returned to New York City, and our text relationship continued. It was clear I needed a change.

Having few friends in New York, and craving something new, I ventured off to Los Angeles for a short break—which was unexpectedly extended into months and, eventually, into a semi-permanent move. And just like that, I found myself living a bicoastal lifestyle, an exciting yet nerve-wracking leap out of my comfort zone. Alex was there for me then, too. We were sexting and talking nonstop during this time. It felt very intimate. He even talked about coming to visit me in L.A. It felt as if this visit would be some sort of trial for our relationship. It's possible that I was delusional, but I'm certain that what we were enacting then was much more than an innocent friendship.

He never did come to visit because, two months later, he met someone else.

Fuuuuck.

Ugh. I thought surely it wasn't going to last. But, slowly, Alex stopped responding to my texts with the frequency I was used to. No more "good nights." No more "good mornings." I know you might be thinking that we were exes, how normal. But we were still doing all of that. It was exactly what I had grown accustomed to over the previous four years post-breakup—or, rather, over the fourteen years of our knowing each other.

This sudden change sent me into a tailspin of PTSD, triggering a depressive episode, something I hadn't experienced since I was a teenager. I was a total mess. It would have been one thing if our texts had continued and he had merely grown distant. But he stopped responding to my messages completely. Once, I (stupidly) inquired about his new relationship, texting something like "Do you love him?" When he texted back "Yes," I was in an anxious state for weeks. I stopped eating and lost seven pounds. I started popping Ativan like candy, and I went back on antidepressants, the same ones I had been off for fifteen years. Hello, Zoloft!

I knew the place I was in. I knew what it was. It was familiar, like an old friend I hadn't seen in years. But I didn't want
to see that old friend. I wanted that friend to go away, and I
wanted Alex to keep talking to me. I wanted him and his new
man to break up. I wanted things to be anything but what they
were. But the harder I resisted the reality, the worse I felt. I sent
him some crazy texts—oopsies again—and eventually things
came to a head.

I finally told him how I was feeling. "I thought we were
going to end up together," I said. "We've been talking every
day. You said you'd come visit me in L.A. And now: nothing. I
barely hear from you."

He acted as if I were crazy. "It's been four years," he said.
"I don't understand where this is coming from."

His genuinely confused tone sent shock waves through my
body. Maybe I had created this whole fantasy in my head. He
seemed to think so. Derek and my friends assured me that, fac-
tually, this was incorrect. They reminded me how much Alex
and I had been talking post-breakup. They reminded me of
the sexts and the videos he had recently sent. The intimacy
had remained. Alex's confusion was the exact type of denial
and inability to discuss present dynamics that had caused me
to end the relationship in the first place. It was almost like
proof or evidence. A big, fat reminder.

I told him I didn't want us to talk anymore. And that was
it. It felt as if we had just broken up again.

I was heartbroken and in a state of grief and denial. My
feelings were also about what losing Alex meant in the context
of my life as a whole. (Remember the discussion of context in
chapter 2? I will remind you here how important it is.)

Whenever you're going through something hard, you must

take into consideration the whole context. Start with your family, then shift toward your friends, work, environment, and beyond. If you're not close with your family, are struggling socially, are on the fence about your job, or hate your home, any loss will feel *very hard*. There are layers or spheres of influence that will exert pressure on certain situations, making them feel more intense. If you sprain your ankle and already have knee problems, the ankle pain will feel worse. The same goes for relationships.

This was my context: I had lost my life partner. I had ended it. I had lost my dog/child Zoey. I had lost my father; he had died. I had lost my brothers. We were estranged. I had few friends in New York City and had just set up a second home in L.A. While I had made several friends, they were all new relationships. My mother was old—still kicking, but older, and unable to be there for me in the ways I wanted. And I was alone.

There was also the even more significant historical context. My childhood had been fraught with instances of abandonment, neglect, abuse, and emotional distress. This had resulted in a pervasive sense of insecurity and instability, which impacted my capacity to feel safe and loved. My family, who ideally should have been my source of love, support, and safety, were instead the instigators of my pain.

The relationship with Alex had provided a form of the love and safety I had craved since childhood. In many ways, Alex was symbolic of the emotional security I had lacked growing up. And now I was grappling with the loss of what Alex had represented: love, safety, acceptance. So, when I recognized that Alex had truly moved on, this exacerbated my feelings of loneliness and rejection, which mirrored the emotional abandonment I had experienced as a child.

My experience with Alex tore open emotions I had suppressed for years, initiating what Derek called an obsessional crisis—a state of intense anxiety and discomfort where unwanted thoughts, impulses, or images consumed me. James Hollis delves deeply into this concept when he says, "What is unconscious remains repressed until activated, at which time it is projected onto another. An obsessional projective identification occurs when the other is charged with carrying our missing piece, thus becoming the carrier of our well-being, or alternatively our greatest threat." Throughout this experience, Alex seemed like he was the missing puzzle piece in my life. It felt as though he had the key to my ability to lead a meaningful life. While incredibly painful, this provided Derek and me an opportunity to delve into what my unconscious mind was attempting to reveal. In our sessions, we reevaluated the importance of my feelings, recognizing them as a projection of past experiences of abandonment and trauma. The task for me, as Hollis and other therapists have been known to say, is to make the unconscious dynamic conscious. Hollis continues, "We are summoned to confront the very thing that was too large for the child to bear or assimilate. It is the reflexive memory of the unbearable quantity of affect that keeps an obsession functioning." As Hollis wisely suggests, I needed to comprehend that as an adult I possessed the capacity to endure what had once felt unbearable. I had to accept what I couldn't as a child: I was, and always had been, alone. Moreover, I had to acknowledge that as an adult my loneliness was fundamentally different from the loneliness in childhood. It was manageable. I no longer needed to harbor the same level of fear that had plagued my entire life.

The night I realized this, I sobbed uncontrollably and for a very long time. In that moment, I was able not only to connect but to feel how it was all related.

The connection I had maintained with Alex in the years following our breakup was undoubtedly fueled by the love I still had for him. But my rigid and unyielding grip on an attachment was about my past trauma and a desperation not to have to face it again. The harder I clung to Alex, the more I could deny the pain of my past and present losses. Trauma is really the gift that keeps on giving.

I've spent decades unpacking and analyzing my trauma. And I've spent decades helping others do the same. Yet the remnants of my past experiences remain. The thing about trauma is, it doesn't just stop. There is no cure; it continues to live within us. It remains within our bodies, often below the level of our consciousness. Like a lingering shadow, it can slip into our present experiences, subtly (or not so subtly) influencing our thoughts, feelings, and actions, even if we're not explicitly thinking about the traumatic events.

It's an ongoing process and working through it can be complex and time-consuming, but it is an essential part of healing and moving forward.

MOVING ON-ISH

Life begins on the other end of despair.

—SARTRE

One month after I ended my relationship, I went to see Esther Perel speak at the 92nd Street Y. She polled the audience, as she always does, asking, "How many of you are in a relationship or married?" For the first time in a long time, this wasn't me. Then she asked, "How many of you are single?" As I raised my hand, a tear ran down my face. I felt vulnerable. It seemed so official.

This may seem overly dramatic, but if you've ever departnered from a long-term relationship, you will know that it is a trauma that requires a major dose of deprogramming. Breakups, even when self-inflicted, are like undergoing open-heart surgery. Nothing prepares you for this type of loss. Culturally, we don't hold space for the complexities of a relationship's ending. Whether family, friend, or partner, we don't acknowledge or honor the depth of such losses. After an ending, getting closure and moving on become the primary focus.

Let's talk about rom-coms for a sec. Romantic comedies often depict a straight woman in the "getting back to me" phase, with men being portrayed as less emotionally complex. The narrative typically involves the woman's taking time for herself, going on a trip, dating again, or experiencing some wacky misadventures before meeting her next partner. Alternatively, she may end up living happily ever after, but alone, in a state of self-acceptance, independence, and strength.

Welp. It's a wonderful fantasy, but it isn't reality.

I was not prepared. I, too, thought it would be a rom-com. I booked retreats. I searched for myself. I practiced yoga. I meditated. I "got back to me." Well, sorta. Ending my relationship forced me to (again) confront a variety of past, present, and future challenges. It was an algebraic equation: Childhood + trauma + being gay + family estrangement/breakup = prolonged grief. What's the equation for your context?

It's usually childhood + trauma + personal identity + social community + career + financial safety + access to resources and healthcare. It is important to acknowledge all the factors present during any life transition, as neglecting one of them could result in leaving out a significant piece of your story.

This isn't some "happily ever after" love story. I've been single since Alex and I broke up. I wanted him back on several occasions, but only when he didn't want me back. I still think about him every day. I still dream about him at night.

I've been alone for a long time. And it's hard.

I have had great success with work. I've made new friends. And my self-confidence? I finally know who I am, am confident, and have landed on a self-definition I can say I genuinely like. But I remain stuck romantically. Everyone I date frustrates me. No one communicates. It seems impossible to get someone interested to the point where they'll stick around. Plus, it's not just other people. It's me. I haven't *felt* something in a long time.

Birthdays and holidays have been absolutely awful. They are only reminders of my loss and loneliness. My first Christmas after breaking up with Alex was terrible. I of course spent it with Alex; we cried. His family expressed their wish that we remain together. Alex and I had sex. It was a mess. Nevertheless, I am glad I spent that time with them. They still felt like my family. *He* still felt like my family.

Subsequent holidays were just as hard. I *dreaded* them. I missed his family (and still do). I missed our routines. I missed having someone to surprise, to go holiday shopping with for cute gifts. To buy beautiful wrapping paper and fancy bows. (I used to go all out.) The absence of such moments had left a void; I missed them dearly. Alex felt the same way, and during these times of the year, my yearning for these shared experiences was particularly acute.

Omg and don't even get me started on Valentine's Day! Alex and I had this tradition where we would make sushi and exchange presents. It was very sweet, and I used to look forward to it. So, I wasn't prepared for what it would be like to be an observer and not a participant on this stupid holiday. It really sucked.

I still miss Alex often. It's not just him that I miss. It's the metaphor. It's the life we had. It's being able to say "we." "We" are doing this, "we" are visiting friends, "we" are going to France this summer. Instead of, "I booked flights alone. I don't know who I am going with yet."

Whenever I talk to people about these feelings, they're quick to say, "Do you think you're over it?" When they do, I'll scream inside while politely saying, "I think so." But my relationship with Alex played such a huge role in my life that I'm not sure how one gets *over* something like that.

I know they're thinking, *Wow, he is still so not over it.*

But we don't get *over* loss; we move *through* it, but the loss stays with us. If you lose a family member, do you simply move on and get over it? No. Your life changes. You add it to your life, and the loss evolves into something smaller and more manageable, something you may not even think about very much. But the loss remains. Alex was my family, and losing him was significant. Will I "move on"? Will meeting someone new alter my perspective on my relationship with him? Undoubtedly, time and new experiences will bring healing and change. Nonetheless, the memories of our time together will always remain with me.

It's undeniably hard to be alone, yet culture, family, and friends rarely provide us with the space to navigate the emotional difficulties that accompany single life. Instead, there are all those reductive phrases that convey implicit judgment—comments like "You should enjoy being single" or "Maybe you need to love yourself more." They are only reminders of society's expectations regarding independence and grief rather than empathy.

Some people do in fact "move on," no longer feeling preoccupied by thoughts of their ex. Others don't. Neither response is inherently "healthier" than the other. You might think, *Well, I would choose never to think about them again.* But our feelings aren't a matter of choice. We have to accept where we are, tolerate it, and resist the urge to judge ourselves against some imagined ideal. It's a flawed assumption to think that if you stop thinking about your ex your life will automatically improve. Life will remain complex and challenging regardless of who occupies your thoughts.

It's often through (not around) pain and heartbreak that we learn the most about ourselves and what it means to be alive. While ending my relationship was difficult, discovering who I was as an independent person without any relationship to shape my identity was even more challenging. This is where I became myself.

BECOMING OURSELVES

The relationship with Alex was a stepping stone to myself. People often talk about "finding themselves," but we don't actually *find* ourselves; we *become* ourselves. And this process of self-discovery continues throughout our entire lifetime, continually unfolding and evolving.

I spent all of my twenties knowing myself as an "us." As a "we."

We just had a relaxing weekend.

We went to a movie.

We will stay in this house for a few more years, sell it, and buy something bigger.

We defined *me.* Before that we, I was me—sad, alone, and traumatized.

When the relationship ended, I was thirty-one. I had no social life because, for so long, I had isolated myself within the relationship. I had a broken relationship with my family, and I was lost professionally. I felt powerless, helpless, desperate to find something to stabilize me the way my relationship always had. But there was nothing.

I felt like a boat adrift in the ocean. "Unmoored," Derek said, and he was right. It felt as if nothing were holding my feet to the ground, that if no one texted me to check in, to say, "When are you coming home for dinner?" I might just drift away.

I hadn't lived alone as a single person in a decade, and living alone is a completely different version of life. There were times I went months without being touched.

Then there were times when I would be touched and it was awful. It's been five years since I heard someone say to me, "I love you." And I haven't expressed love to anyone, either. I'm not sure which is worse.

Single people aren't allowed to acknowledge the profound absence of love. They aren't even allowed to admit it to themselves.

But it wasn't all doom and gloom. Suddenly, I didn't have to be accountable to anyone but myself. I could be whoever I wanted to be. I didn't have to feel guilty, or as if I were betraying anyone or anything just to express myself. If I wanted to eat dinner at five and go to bed at eight-thirty, I could, and did. If I wanted to masturbate for an hour, I could. That's not to say I didn't do these things in my relationship. But when you're in a relationship, there is always a delicate dance around compromise, and sometimes we refrain from doing certain things in order to remain connected to our partner.

After Alex, I grew up, in every way possible. I grew tremendously professionally, and I created a whole new life out of thin air—and that has been empowering AF, something else no one ever recognizes: People should be celebrated for rebuilding their lives after this kind of loss.

Though it certainly would be nice if we spent more time acknowledging this, because the efforts one must make after a breakup are truly herculean. The reward, of course, is inner peace.

YOU DESERVE ACKNOWLEDGMENT

If you're on the other side of a breakup, you deserve a medal.

I hope you feel proud of the effort you've put into recovering and rebuilding. I'll assume no one has told you this, but you should feel really fucking proud. I know how hard it is; it's a huge accomplishment. Take a moment to really celebrate it.

And if you have a friend going through a breakup, make sure you regularly (like, exaggeratedly) tell them how impressed you are with them, how proud you are of how hard they're pushing themselves.

I'm not just saying this to pump you up, but because it is true. Ending a relationship, going through that loss, and building a new life for yourself is really hard work. Acknowledge it.

Still, I found it challenging to rebuild my social life. During my relationship, I had spent so much time retreating into the wonderful parts, or feeling consumed by the difficult ones, that my priority at the time became nourishing the relationship. And I was good at it. As a consequence, though, I neglected other aspects of my life, particularly my social life outside the relationship. I now know how important it is to have a life outside your relationship, but back then, I honestly didn't want one. I genuinely wanted to spend time with Alex. Even if you don't want to socialize with others, you must. Because when—not if—your relationship becomes challenging, you will have nothing and no one to lean on for support or fun.

When things ended with Alex, I knew that making new friends would be my first step. And while, at the time, I wouldn't have admitted this, I was scared. Making new friends as an adult is majorly difficult. Let me say it again: It's fucking hard.

I had maintained the few friends I had from my undergrad days at NYU, but I had never ventured out toward a larger community. So when I became single, I was socially isolated.

In New York City, everyone is busy with a capital *B*. Their social, professional, and travel schedules barely leave room for their own self-care, let alone socializing with a new friend. And if, like me, you're an introvert, go to bed early, hate bars and clubs, and drink very little, it's even harder. Everyone I met wanted to get dinner at 8 P.M. or go out at 9 to grab a drink. Meanwhile, I am a grandparent who goes to bed at 9:30, so neither option is possible. In the beginning, I would oblige their schedule and end up in a constant state of exhaustion. But as time passed, I simply declined.

Logistics aside, I learned an important lesson about myself and my friends. For a large portion of my life I had a narrative that went something like this: "I like to relax at home alone. It feels comfortable, and I don't need to see anyone. People are annoying and don't understand me. I'm totally fine. I'm entirely satisfied with chilling at home." But the reality was, I wasn't fine. It was yet another extension of the personality I had developed in the face of chronic family disappointment and loss. The reality was, I had found it difficult to establish trust and security within all relationships. This was a struggle I had had since childhood, when safety proved to be an unreliable resource in my family.

As American psychiatrist Peter Kramer writes, "What appears to be a problem in socializing is really a problem in mood." This applied to me then, but at the time, I would never have been able to acknowledge it. Why? Because in my conscious awareness, I looked forward to, almost desperately craved, alone time. But I started to notice that by day five of being alone, the solitude was no longer a treat. It became a way to numb myself, and it was not easing my tension or sadness, but maintaining it. Maybe even creating it!

Luckily, I had the opportunity to challenge the (rigid) belief that had persisted since childhood about requiring distance from others for peace and quiet. It turns out I was completely wrong. I hadn't been luxuriating in my alone time, but *hiding*. This is when I stepped out of my comfort zone and began to participate in activities I never thought I would have the desire, courage, or ability to do.

I made many new friends, and you know what? I *loved* them. I began to prefer hanging out with them to spending time alone. Don't get me wrong—I still love and need my alone time. But being social is now rewarding and enjoyable. It's a balance.

We all have narratives about the things we like and don't like. Often, these narratives are shaped by trauma and our fears, or by adaptive strategies we've developed over time to protect ourselves from pain. Whether it's specific activities or our desire for togetherness versus being alone, I would deeply encourage you to challenge these narratives at least a few times. Get outside your comfort zone. Shake things up every once in a while.

I guarantee you, it's better to discover you've been wrong about yourself than to regret it years down the line.

As I was learning the importance of pushing myself out-side my comfort zone and toward more social and romantic risks, my clients were doing the same. This was particularly so for John, a client I had seen for many years.

JOHN: FEELINGS ARE NOT ALWAYS VALID

John first began therapy with me seven years ago. A thirty-eight-year-old African cisgender male who identifies as gay, he had recently started a new business. Stressed and majorly depressed, he was miserable. And for good reason. His life, for all intents and purposes, was miserable. When I asked why he wanted to be in therapy, he said, "There is nothing specific. I just know I need to be in therapy"—something I've heard from many clients. I knew there would be a lot to unpack once he opened up.

John initially appeared withdrawn and emotionally flat in our sessions. I wanted to make him smile, so I would often use humor and sarcasm. It did the trick, sometimes. John had experienced multiple traumas in his life. Born in Nigeria, he was separated from his mother, culture, and familiar surroundings when, at the age of six, he immigrated (without notice) to North Carolina.

Transitioning to life in the United States had been an uphill battle for John, who faced a complex mix of challenges stemming from racial, cultural, and religious disparities, and feelings of isolation and loneliness. And rightfully so. I can't imagine immigrating to a foreign country as an adult, let alone as a child. In North Carolina, John found himself navigating a cultural divide that was almost as wide as the geographical one he had crossed.

North Carolina presented an array of new social norms, expectations, and practices that were starkly different from those he had known in his native Nigeria. These contrasts were not merely superficial; they touched every aspect of his life, presenting John with a set of challenges that tested his adaptability and resilience.

In Nigeria, John had lived in a predominantly Black community, where he blended in with his peers and felt a strong sense of belonging. His transition to a largely white neighborhood in the United States had therefore marked a significant shift in his racial experience. Suddenly, he found himself in the minority, standing out in ways he never had back home.

Navigating racial dynamics in the United States, with its long and painful history of slavery and racial discrimination, was a new reality for John. He had to grapple with racial prejudice and stereotypes he had never encountered in Africa. His skin color, which had been a nonissue in his home country, suddenly became a focus of attention, bias, and misunderstanding. This marked difference between his racial experiences in Nigeria and the United States profoundly impacted his sense of identity and belonging.

At six years old, John did his best to navigate these new dynamics, but without the help of his parents, he struggled. His family was absent in every way possible, whether that was demonstrated by their serving him food they knew he was allergic to or not showing any meaningful curiosity as to why John was struggling.

As he grew older, he realized that he was gay, which his father didn't accept. This led to more rejection, criticism, and conflict. Once John left his family, he retreated inward for over a decade for self-protecting, becoming isolated.

John's self-blame and shame was overwhelming. In session, he and I dedicated significant time and effort to reshaping his narrative into something softer, something that involved the compassion and acceptance he had lacked during childhood.

While John made progress in reducing his shame, increasing his self-esteem, and improving his self-care, he remained stuck socially and romantically. With only two friends, no dating experience, and a complete avoidance of sex, he unconsciously communicated that he was closed for all kinds of business—other than his actual business. John became a workaholic, taking on excessive work that overwhelmed him.

In the process of therapy (at least with me), repeated convincing and positive reinforcement often play crucial roles in
my clients' healing. But, for people to truly believe they deserve
love, they must experience it—mere verbal affirmation may
not suffice.

Lightbulbs don't go off just because someone tells us we
deserve love and happiness. We have to *believe* it, and in order
to develop that belief, we have to *experience* that love and happiness. John, for instance, shied away from relationships, an
unconscious expression of the fears rooted in his childhood,
which he consciously translated into a preference for solitude—
much like my own. In therapy, he became a bit stuck. Lacking
any relational connection, he had difficulty embracing and
internalizing his newfound insights related to self-care, self-
love, and compassion.

He needed connection and shared joy to understand not
only that he was likable but that he would also like others and
feel safe. And that's the thing: John was *extremely* likable. He
was kind, funny, stylish, talented, smart, and, despite his automatic reflex to hide, very personable and relationally oriented.
Many of my clients are truly wonderful people who, due to
their traumas, are blind to how wonderful they actually are. I
think to some extent we all are.

Slowly but surely, I convinced John that work maybe wasn't
more important than relationships. I then started pushing him
to do social things, to be out in the community—whether that
meant reaching out to friends and acquaintances or attending
art classes in the city. This took months, but then one day, I
received a text message from John. It was a picture of a clay
pot. I knew right away what this meant: *John had gone to a pottery class!* And of course, like everything he did, his work was

exquisite. I think I was happier than he was. When we talked about his new hobby in session, he said he had enjoyed the course—that it was fun—and that he was going to another class that week.

For John, the pottery course wasn't just a pottery course. It was John testing the boundaries of the defense mechanisms that had kept him far out of social reach. Soon after, he started reaching out to friends, and while he wasn't head over heels about doing so, he admitted that it had been "nice" and that he had had some "fun."

"Nice and fun! I'll take it," I joked with a big smile on my face. He smiled, too.

The point here is that John's life was stuck not because of his trauma per se but because of the defenses he had developed in response to that trauma, which were ongoing in his mind and body. The only way he was able to heal from those earlier experiences was to have completely new, contrasting experiences in the here and now.

John challenged himself. I challenged myself. And I want you to challenge yourself, too.

When you've lived through trauma, your mind and body can play tricks on you. Your body might react with fear and anxiety, trying its best to prevent you from doing exactly what might be most beneficial for you. It's essential to question and challenge these automatic reactions, as daunting as this may be. Yes, confronting your fears can be frightening in and of itself, but what's even more frightening is spending an adulthood that parallels the loneliness of your childhood. This is an example of another way we can experience a sort of second childhood in our adult lives. As discussed in chapter 6, these parallels to childhood frequently surface within the dynamics of our relationships or in the absence of relationships.

The most significant hurdle to recognizing our wounds and how they are triggered is a lack of self-awareness. However, there are always unconscious elements that can prevent us from developing the self-awareness necessary to create the change we seek. The key to making the unconscious conscious lies in observing our behaviors, understanding their outcomes, and identifying recurring patterns.

In both John's case and mine, we found comfort in solitude, often finding others more bothersome than beneficial. The consequence of this was not the peace we sought but loneliness. More often than not, withdrawal serves as a defense mechanism. It's the way we protect ourselves. Whether withdrawing from social situations, or even during a single conversation, you can be sure that doing so reflects some level of self-protection. However, this tactic, while perhaps effective in our childhood, only results in feelings of a terminal sense of loneliness and hopelessness in adulthood.

OUR EMOTIONS ARE COMPLEX

At times our feelings are more about the past than the present.

I urge you to scrutinize them (not too much, though) and test their limitations. When I say "scrutinize," I don't mean doubt or question the validity of an emotional experience. Many of us often think, *Should I be feeling this?* or express confusion: *I shouldn't feel this way, I don't understand.* The question we should be asking is not whether we should or shouldn't feel a certain way, but rather *why* we feel the way we do. What's the narrative behind it? Never doubt your emotions. Instead, look into their origin. Your emotions hold significant value.

This is particularly noticeable when it comes to dating. I've worked with several clients who longed for relationships, yet had a strong aversion to the dating process. The mere thought of downloading a dating app could trigger a wide range of emotional responses. They harbored beliefs about dating being a pointless exercise, about people being disappointing (which they can be), about dating apps being flawed (they are), and countless other reasons to avoid going on dates. But at its core, while there is some truth, the avoidance is more about fear: fear of rejection, fear of disappointment, and fear of the unknown. But that's exactly when we need to push ourselves, to question our apprehension and not blindly accept everything our minds tell us.

DATING

When my relationship ended, I thought I would have single life figured out and my future planned.

I would be single.

Slut it up.

Eventually, I'd start dating. Then I'd fall in love, establish a new relationship, quickly move in with him, and have a child. *After all, I'm not a monster,* I thought. *I'm nice, cute, and quite good at relationships. (Hello! it's what I do for a living.) How hard could it be?* (Lol I'm laughing and crying inside as I write this because nothing has been further from the truth.)

I was not prepared for the circus of dating and the single

life. I had heard anecdotes from clients and friends, but I hadn't experienced firsthand since I was a teenager what it was like to be single. And I'm not sure that counts.

One evening, I was talking to someone on the dating app Hinge and I asked my usual questions, the most important one being "What are you looking for?"

DON'T WAIT: HAVE ALL THE TALKS

This is for single people and couples. Ask questions right from the beginning. Build a culture of open and direct communication from the start. This will make it easier to have these conversations years later—if you get there.

But always ask, "What are you looking for?" Right from the beginning. And then check in with your partner about how the relationship is going for them. For some reason, people have developed intense anxiety and fear around being the one to have "the Talk." Defining or redefining the relationship is actually an important factor of relational health. You're not being too needy for wanting to make sure yours and your new partner's goals are aligned. Rest assured, seeking clarity and alignment of goals doesn't make you excessively demanding. On the contrary, it's a crucial skill that reflects bravery, intellect, and emotional maturity. If your partner struggles to receive or respond to your communication, it's important to remember that their difficulties are not a reflection of you. Their resistance is not a Stop sign or an indicator that you're

wrong or bad. It's merely an expression of difference.
Keep talking.

He said, "I am one hundred percent looking for a relationship, but I'm not desperate for one; I'm still trying to figure out
what I want in a partner."

While this was not a terrible response, the relational expert
in me was instantly turned off by the avoidance implied by his
need to disclose a lack of desperation. I felt immediately self-
conscious: Unlike him, I *was* desperate. When I considered my
response to what he'd said, my feeling turned off: *Wow, how
interesting!,* I thought. *Can we even know what we want in a partner
before having met him?*

Abso-fucking-lutely not!

Needless to say, we spoke for a few moments, but I
decided to unmatch with him. Since re-entering the dating scene, I had continually found myself confronted with
evasive and indirect responses regarding relationship goals
and desires. Initially, I chose to engage with these men, only
to discover that subsequent answers to my questions were
equally defensive and lacking in vulnerability. I know. It's
hard to admit to a stranger that you are in search of love,
and long for it. But that is my truth—I am seeking love and
I do yearn for it deeply.

My decision was to stop entertaining individuals who
weren't up-front about their intent to pursue a committed
relationship. I stopped investing my time in those who didn't
explicitly express a desire for a partnership. I made this choice
for my own well-being, but it is not necessarily a universal

choice or the "right" way to date; it is simply what worked best for me.

Admittedly, my approach is based on my biases and assumptions. For example, he *did* say he was looking for a relationship. However, his declaration of being happy on his own or not desperately seeking a relationship rubbed me the wrong way. It's possible that he would eventually have let his guard down, and perhaps I missed out on a potential love connection. Regardless, it's the path I chose.

The key is to find what works best for you. Ideally, the more open and transparent you can be before meeting someone in person, the better. However, it's important to remember that it's okay to have thoughts and subsequent reactions when faced with a lack of emotional availability.

Undoubtedly, dating has its benefits. I've discovered many valuable things. I learned how to select the perfect paint color for my living room (Chelsea Grey) and how to secure discounts at designer stores. During a recent date, I was so enamored of shoes the guy was wearing that I purchased a pair for myself, which I now fucking love. I've also formed some wonderful friendships through dating; at least three of my close friends started off as dates. If I hadn't exposed myself to this new experience, I never would have learned about these beautiful things or acquired these lovely friendships.

I encourage you to consider your own, different approach to dating, too. Instead of going on dates with the expectation that the other person will be "the One"—an expectation that, as we covered in chapter 2, often leads to disappointment—try to adopt a more open-minded perspective.

Let's establish a new rule: Dating should be viewed as an

opportunity for new experiences, whether relational, inter-personal, or intrapersonal (as in the relationship we have with ourselves). Sure, with every first date, we naturally hope for a meaningful connection, but we should also be open to learning from each new potential partner we meet, whether or not it results in a relationship.

Whatever you do, do not play games. Get attached. Develop feelings. Do it all! It's okay to cling. In fact . . .

DON'T STOP BEING CLINGY

If anything, I wish we could start a cultural movement encouraging people to cling *more*. People are too avoidant, unavailable, shut down. They don't cling enough. They play it too cool. They act aloof, and take other estranged and anti-relational stances. Many of my single clients are either trying to date people like this or are those people themselves. Yes, relationships are inherently scary; they're full of risk. And there has been so much disinformation out there. The number of blog posts from *BuzzFeed*, *The Cut*, and *Cosmo* instructing people on how *not* to catch feelings, how to play it cool, and other topics is shocking.

But I believe the desire for deep attachment is a *strength*. So, if you do, too, I commend your capacity for love and attachment. It is a valuable skill. Don't give it up in response to social pressure or discouragement.

Being alone is currently sold as this golden prize. People are told they need to love themselves first, and better. They're told to leave a "bad" relationship as the bar for "good" ones is placed higher and higher. We are told to enjoy being single. I think this is bullshit. Being alone is hard, and this kind of thinking only minimizes our feelings, our desire for connection. Not that you can't enjoy being single; you can. But we shouldn't be approaching our lives with the belief that we should.

Some people are perfectly content whether they are single or in a relationship. But many people *really* want a relationship and are often criticized and shamed. We are told a range of dismissive statements like "If you can't be happy single, you won't be happy in a relationship" to "Do you want to be in a relationship, or are you just lonely?"—as if to say you can't be lonely *and* be seeking companionship.

There is an idea about being our "best self" and creating the perfect internal state before dating or entering a relationship. Those who are newly single are discouraged from "jumping" into a new relationship. Friends and family tell them, "Stay single! Wait until you meet the One . . . until you are healed . . . until you are ready . . . blah blah blah." It's as if getting into a relationship were akin to signing your house away!

I believe that everyone is "relationship-ready" and should settle *down* (not for less and not for a bad relationship). Do it for the experience, for the self-awareness and growth! Do it for fun. Our culture has a bad habit of slapping labels on us as we search for love: "anxious," "avoidant," "clingy," "co-dependent," "desperate," "not ready," "damaged," "serial monogamist." Guess what? Even if you're all those things, you are also "relationship-ready."

So, get into that relationship! Remember, you can always end it if it doesn't work. And in the process, you will grow more than if you had simply stayed single, forever looking for someone perfect who—surprise—does not exist. Shift your thinking away from the cliché advice the lovelorn are always given and, instead, focus on yourself and your partner. Learn about each other's lives. Become aware. Prepare for challenges. Work through conflicts. Negotiate differences. Have sex.

Have a relationship.

Everyone's a Little Unhealthy

The curious paradox is that when I accept myself just
as I am, then I can change.

—Carl Rogers

BEING A THERAPIST

I'm often amused to see a client's surprise when they discover
I also have my own struggles. But therapists, like anyone else,
have their own challenges and imperfections. As meditation
teacher and writer Sharon Salzberg wisely expressed, "My suffering might even be my credential." I believe mine is.

Yet therapists are often objectified, first by their training
institutions and peers, then by themselves and their friends,
and ultimately by their clients. This objectification can foster

an illusion that therapists are infallible, almost superhuman, creating unrealistic expectations and pressures. It also often overlooks the fact that therapists navigate their own ups and downs. Ironically, even therapists need therapists.

During my time in graduate school, we were advised against self-disclosure to clients, a guideline I found myself instinctively challenging. Initially, I followed the rules. Then, I quickly said, "Fuck it." Why bother? It wasn't who I was. I am a very open person, and much of my growth as a therapist (and human being) stems from my personal journey—not from the abnormal psychology textbook I had to memorize in grad school.

In discussing the therapist-client relationship, Carl Rogers says, "It is only by providing the genuine reality, which is in me, that the other person can successfully seek for the reality in him." I do just this; by offering my authentic self in session, my clients are able to explore their own realities safely and more effectively. I don't sit in silence. I don't spend a session processing and analyzing where my clients sit in the office or from what room in their home they are Zooming me. I offer guidance and advice to my clients. Sometimes I can take a more active role during sessions by encouraging clients to address tasks they've been avoiding. For instance, I once assisted a client in scheduling a long-overdue doctor's appointment, and in other sessions, I've helped clients send messages on dating apps. This hands-on approach allows clients to confront their fears in a safe and supportive environment, not just in processing them but in actually overcoming them.

I don't have rigid boundaries regarding self-disclosure. Obviously, I do not spend an entire session talking about my father, but I do add personal snippets here and there.

I also joke and try to make my clients laugh.

I offer contact outside of sessions. We all use text and email daily to augment communication in our relationships. I do it with Derek, and during times of crisis, it has been beyond helpful.

I'm a human being. What you see in me in session is very similar to who I am outside it—maybe minus the socially awkward side that comes out when I'm in crowds.

My clients always say, "That's your *therapist* response. What do *you* think?" I always laugh at this one. There is no difference.

My clients help me just as much as I help them. Derek once said to me that being a therapist is like having thirty hours of personal therapy each week. What he meant is that as therapists we can learn about ourselves in sessions with our clients—that is, if you're open to learning about your own stuff. And boy, did I learn!

I conduct therapy like a relationship, in the hope that my clients (and I) will use the template I provide, generalizing it to other relational contexts. Over the course of twenty-five years, my own personal journey in therapy brought about significant changes within me. However, it wasn't solely insights or attachment theory that facilitated this transformation; it was the profoundly loving relationship I shared with my therapist, Derek. His impact has not only changed (saved) my life but continues to influence every session with my own clients and even in the content of what I'm writing to you.

While most people want catharsis or profound revelations from therapy, research has shown that the most significant factor for successful therapeutic outcomes is the alliance between the therapist and the client. Yes, gaining insights and understanding is an essential aspect of therapy, but it is the relationship between these two parties that, for decades, has been widely documented as the most impactful. All studies have shown that this relationship is a stronger predictor of positive outcomes than any one specific modality or intervention: not the therapeutic orientation; not cognitive behavioral therapy, dialectical behavioral therapy, Internal Family Systems, or any other therapeutic perspectives; not re-parenting; not self-love; not attachment style. But relational love.

All traumas are fundamentally relationally rooted, and as a result, the path to healing must also involve relational experiences. This is the essence of the corrective emotional experience I discussed in chapter 6, and it represents the primary objective in therapy within the therapist-client relationship. I recall a session I had with Derek: I was (very) late, panic set in. I feared Derek would be as upset with me as my father had been with any of my mistakes or missteps. Arriving at his office, I remained anxious. Derek picked up on my distress and reassured me that lateness had no bearing on how he felt toward me, and that it's normal (duh). Although it may appear simplistic, Derek modeled a new relational dynamic that directly challenged the fears rooted in my original trauma with my father. I realized that I could make mistakes, even be late, and still be graded in a positive light. This experience served as a corrective emotional experience for me. Peter Levine writes, "The purpose of the very act of recall is to provide the molecular opportunity to update memory based upon new information. This is, in other words, the essence of not only how the past persists in the present, but how the present has the potentiality of changing (what was) the past." Therapy helps us update our memories and interrupt the repetition of early patterns. This is why positive outcomes in our life will be reflected in the quality of our relationships. Not analyzing toxic behaviors or any other buzzwords you learned on the internet. It comes from having better relationships. It comes from having repeated corrective relational experiences with others. This is how we change our lives. If you love yourself, but your relationships are a mess—what's the point? And no, self-love doesn't automatically convert to relational skills. It is our relationships that define whether a life is worth living.

Don't get me wrong. One of the most important relationships we have is with ourselves. But that relationship, just like relationships with others, is just as impermanent and imperfect.

EVERYONE'S A LITTLE UNHEALTHY

Being a therapist is an interesting experience. I've spent thousands of hours listening to people talk about their inner worlds. Sometimes I know more about my clients than their spouses or best friends.

Therapy is a unique place. It's a space where people can access support and attention, all without the reciprocal obligations inherent in most of our other relationships. For some, it is a sanctuary for self-reflection and healing. However, for others, it's an uncomfortable and confusing place that brings about deep discomfort. I see people as they are, not for who they pretend to be or are fearful of revealing. And when that fear comes up in session, we talk about it.

This is a unique perspective, one few people get. As a therapist, I'm able to see, again and again, how relational approaches play out over time. I get to see the starring role that uncertainty plays in the things we all want to be certain: I hear the stories that tell me why that "toxic" person ghosted. I hear people who can't stop berating or shaming themselves for normal mistakes. I hear them obsessing over the unavailability of their partners and over the thousands of Instagram posts that encourage them to "cut him out of your life." I hear why a client's partner has been avoiding sex. I hear it all.

And what I can tell you is this: We will all, at some point, do things we wish we hadn't.

We will all, at some point, lash out when we should show compassion.

We will all ignore, avoid, or desperately obsess until we can no longer bear it and will make major mistakes in our relationships.

Everyone, *every single person,* is a little bit unhealthy. Our mind and body were not designed to fulfill the idealistic standards set by the medical or therapeutic community. We're imperfect. Which means we will never meet all the qualifications in those checklists you see online.

Why is this important? Because everyone's behavior, even when it appears unhealthy, can make perfect sense when we understand their personal story. And this comprehension paves the way for empathy and compassion.

I was perusing a popular Instagram account yesterday while getting my steps in on the treadmill, and I found myself screenshotting post after post, thinking, *Yes. Omg. Sooo good.* Later, I looked at all my screenshots: They were all empowering phrases that *sounded* wonderful. They were sound bites, one-liners. Easy enough? Not so much. I realized how much of an emotional bypass all this "amazing" content was. It *sounds* good, *looks* good, but it minimizes the lived experience we all go through when we can't simply stop, cut someone out, or do what we are being told we should be doing. Human beings don't work like that.

AGNES: "I CAN'T STOP BEING MEAN TO MYSELF"

Agnes, a forty-year-old straight cisgender woman, recently moved from Sweden and entered therapy to work through debilitating loneliness. What I quickly discovered was that underneath that loneliness was a profound sense of shame. Agnes grew up with an incredibly demeaning and critical father who would tell her she was fat and that if she didn't lose weight no one would want her. She had a good relationship with her mother; unfortunately, her mother was unable to protect Agnes from her father's harsh and abusive criticisms. Agnes had one intimate relationship with a partner who sounded just as cruel as her father had been. Beyond this, she had had no experiences with someone being affirming of her. As a result, she developed an inner world that paralleled the treatment she had received from her father and romantic partner. The internal narrative was of self-criticism and uncontrollable shame. She even took it upon herself to feel responsible when a flight she was taking was delayed.

One session, she actually said, *I can't stop being mean to myself.*

When I heard this, it was as if someone had slammed on the brakes. There were many directions in which I could take this remark and a lot to unpack. I paused to think. Then I did a very typical therapist thing and repeated out loud what she had just said: "'I can't stop being mean to myself.' Whoa."

Then I remembered an experience I had had earlier in the week, when I couldn't stop thinking about Alex. I wanted to stop, but my mind kept going back to him. When this happens, I know it's one part my missing Alex, but a bigger part my earlier traumas and overall sense of loneliness in the world. I realized then that Agnes was talking about a similar expression of what I, too, had experienced.

We can't simply stop doing things. And maybe we shouldn't. Agnes grew up in a family that routinely minimized, gaslit, and said terribly cruel things to her. So, she learned at a very young age to turn her negative emotions against herself. Just as I had learned at a very young age to feel scared of being alone. And just as I ruminated over my relationship with Alex to manage my fear of being alone, Agnes was obsessing over what an awful person she was to manage her loneliness. But if stopping unhealthy behaviors were simple, people would have already done it.

This kind of fixation often leads people to perform compulsive actions or rituals. They do this in an attempt to prevent or negate the adverse outcomes they associate with their obsessive thoughts. I've experienced this myself, and I suspect you might relate to it as well.

I am a therapist, and I'm writing a book on relationships— and it's still hard. Why? Because when you're in it, all bets are off, and all trauma responses are on. It's one thing to judge someone else's experience from an unemotional, objective place, to make an Instagram post with a list of ten red flags. But when you're the person desperately craving love, it's a different thing entirely.

Agnes's breakthrough moment wasn't in the complete reduction of her obsessions. (Nor was mine, nor will yours be.) It was, instead, in her recognizing how powerful these experiences can become and learning how to manage and tolerate their intensity.

It's quite remarkable, when you think about it. *We* are quite remarkable—*you* are remarkable! Even when you falter.

Emotional, relational, mental, and sexual health are just like physical health, yet we approach love and relationships

much differently than we do illness. We don't criticize someone who's depressed or yell at a diabetic. But when it comes to
our relationships, one mistake can feel like catastrophic failure.
We can feel abandoned and overwrought with guilt, shame,
and fear—as if we're not supposed to struggle or as if we're
supposed to always do the "right" thing every time we act or
speak. That simply can't happen.

Just like physical health. Just like the weather. We will all
be unhealthy. Life is extremely hard; the pressures our society
places on individuals and couples are greater than ever. The
world is a mess. The environments we live in don't help us
develop healthy lifestyles or relationships. The individualistic,
capitalist society we live in does nothing but prioritize superficial definitions of success at the expense of our health. So, to
expect constant relational health is a fantasy, one incongruent
with our very unhealthy society.

No relationship can measure up to the perfectionistic standards asked of modern love. All relationships will face challenges and could easily be judged as unhealthy by unthinking
outsiders. We will always confront, manage, or tolerate some
dissatisfaction or disappointment.

What fascinates me (and I hope you as well) is the enormous pressure placed on people to have healthy, satisfying relationships without their ever having learned how to cultivate
relational health. And sex, too! Without real sex education,
most people are left to figure out sex from the unrealistic standards set by porn. Let that sink in for a bit. What a mindfuck!
Leaving it to porn to teach the public about sex is like expect-
ing a newborn to start walking immediately or to arrive with a
built-in understanding of mathematics. It's crazy!

In relationships, we're all babies learning how to walk—

except in the case of love relationships, we must effectively communicate and understand how our past traumas surface in the space between ourselves and others. You'd think it would be simple, but due to a little thing called trauma, our feelings often take over and cause us to stumble and fall.

We can't describe our relationships as healthy unless we put in the work to develop self-understanding, relational well-being, and the skills to "do" intimacy. But again, no one teaches us this. There is no "relationship curriculum" in our early school years. Even in college, there is no relationship guidance. This is why people are turning to Instagram and other online platforms for this support. They're the only place where you can get easy access to such advice. (The only other place is from our families, the people who raised us. And I don't know about you, but what I observed in my parents was anything but aspirational.)

Everyone has limitations. Everyone is deeply flawed. Every relationship is imperfect.

We may feel hatred for our partner at times—or what Terry Real refers to as "normal marital hate." It makes me giggle just writing it. It also makes me sad, because if I had had a better understanding of how normal it was to struggle with a partner, my perspective on Alex would have been different.

I have the cutest dog ever, and sometimes—omg I can't believe I'm going to say this—I hate her. Normally, Elly is a super chill, cuddly lapdog. But when someone new comes over (usually a guy I'm giving my attention to), she *freaks out*. She'll bark, pant, jump on the guy's lap, and stare at me, preventing me from touching him. Such a cock-block. It drives me crazy. But I love her to absolute death!

How do you think you would experience yourself if you

expected massive challenges? How do you think you would experience your relationship differently if you knew bad days were coming? That your partner will annoy you? That anyone and everyone will irritate you? Could you tolerate relationship challenges as you would bad weather, knowing that it, too, will pass? I'm not encouraging you to be explicitly unhealthy. But be sure to distinguish between annoyance, frustration, and disappointment and mistreatment or abuse. I'm encouraging you to accept that when—not if—you struggle, it's okay. It's actually healthy, at times, to be unhealthy. In fact, I would go so far as to say that people who do not struggle are deeply emotionally repressed, and this is a major barrier to the relational and sexual experiences in their life.

You'd be surprised how much easier change becomes when you're able to grasp and accept the imperfect predicament of being human.

11

Give Up Hope

Real love allows for failure and suffering.

—Sharon Salzberg

Emotional pain is relational pain. People frequently associate happiness, contentment, and fulfillment in life with the absence of pain or challenges. But the reality is that the more we avoid pain, the *less* fulfilled we become.

The philosophical journey of life's drama unfolds in the context of our relationships. We've already talked about how important pain is to our lives; this applies also to our relationships. The importance of relational challenges, which at first may appear outrageous, requires more reflection. Keep in mind that when I say "pain," I'm not talking about abusive or deeply unsatisfying relationships. Instead, I am referring to anxiety, sadness, or disappointment.

Disappointments and conflicts are not merely obstacles but, rather, necessary components of any relationship and life itself. Doubt, uncertainty, and disagreement serve as catalysts for change and therefore growth. In our most profound relationships, we encounter the task of embracing the seemingly insurmountable, mustering the courage to confront the anxiety stemming from the dissonance between ourselves and our partners. Within this intricate dance, we can only grow. A healthy relationship can only thrive when individuals approach the negotiating table as their authentic selves, demonstrating the bravery to embrace challenges without retreat. It is in this process of rupture and repair, in all our relationships, that we heal.

However, it is important to acknowledge that if disappointment and conflict are mishandled or avoided, which frequently occurs, they can result in detrimental consequences. Poor communication, unwarranted criticisms, the escalation of conflicts, the emergence of hostility, expressions of contempt, and resorting to name-calling can drive wedges between partners, ultimately leading to feelings of resentment and dissatisfaction.

REALITY SUCKS SOMETIMES, AND THAT'S OKAY

If I haven't already completely disappointed you, brace yourself, because I'm about to unleash the biggest bummer of all: Happiness isn't the ultimate goal in life; it's meaning that holds the most significance. As Aldo Carotenuto puts it, "Psychological work, instead of providing liberation from the cause of serious discomfort, increases it, teaching the patient to become adult and, for the first time in his life, actively face the feeling of being alone with his pain and abandoned by the world."

While this may not be the most uplifting quote, it emphasizes a crucial point we must all strive to acknowledge. Essentially, the more we avoid our pain by idealizing states of healing, cure-alls, and perpetual happiness, the less capable we become of embracing ourselves and others. This process hinders our capacity to tolerate, endure, and ultimately grow. It's about recognizing the freedom inherent in taking personal responsibility for our path and accepting the inherent limitations that exist in all living beings.

When we refuse to accept that suffering is a part of being human and try to avoid pain, it only makes it harder for us to feel pleasurable emotions. It also makes us feel guilty and afraid when we inevitably experience challenges, stress, pain, or suffering. We begin to understand common mistakes, or "the small things," as failures—something that happened because of who we are or what we did—which can lead to a sense of inadequacy, as if we have failed at life in general. I've seen this in every client I've treated.

Every one of my clients enters therapy convinced that their particular emotional and relationship struggles are a reflection of their individual defects and inadequacies. In session, we work toward recognizing how certain challenges not only are a natural part of the human experience but also should be expected when we consider our specific life context(s) that contribute to present challenges.

That the Danish philosopher Søren Kierkegaard said, "Life is not a problem to be solved, but a reality to be experienced," reminds us that life isn't about solving every issue in an endless quest for happiness. Instead, we should welcome the diverse experiences it offers us. And I agree. I've been in therapy for almost my entire life, and I'm so over having to watch out for emotional land mines. I don't want to have to keep doing this emotional karate just to make sure I don't spiral out of control.

But . . . I also don't want to live in a fantasyland. In our search for happiness and satisfaction, we often look for solutions to our discomfort or dissatisfaction in an obsessive and anxious way. Most people want to find a way *around* challenges. Few people actually want to face their problems and work through them. We all want our lives and relationships to be free of anxiety and sadness. Contrary to most self-help and psychological advice, Buddhist teacher Pema Chödrön says, "Run toward pain." Which I *fucking love*! Of course, she is not suggesting that people purposely seek out situations that cause suffering or harm. Instead, she means that instead of avoiding or suppressing hard feelings, we should actively deal with them. Similar to Kierkegaard, she says we need to face and accept hard things in order to learn and grow.

Chödrön's idea of running toward pain is a response to her advice to let go of hope. Reading this deeply resonated with me. I quickly realized that the majority of what made me depressed or anxious was a reflex to cling to the hope of something that isn't, wasn't, or could never be.

It shouldn't be like this. (We should still be together.)
I shouldn't be like this. (He shouldn't be in a relationship with someone
    else.)
He shouldn't be like this. (How does he not understand me?)

When will it go away? (When will I stop thinking about him?)

When will it stop? (When will I stop feeling so much pain and loss?)

Will things ever be different? (Am I ever going to fall in love again?)

Tomorrow I will start. (I am too scared and overwhelmed today.)

Next year will be better. (I'm trying to be hopeful and can't tolerate my pain in the present.)

We organize our lives around the hope and a desire for change. We are so fixated on, and invested in, the fantasy of a better future, that we miss experiencing the present.

If you hope for a controllable life free of pain, you'll encounter threats to your stability around every corner, all the time. This mindset can lead to anxiety. Peace comes from understanding that you're capable of recognizing, tolerating, and working through pain when it arises. It's about having faith in your own resilience and your ability to recover.

This isn't an individual problem. It's a cultural problem. You've been *trained* by your culture to think like this. We have all been. And we apply this line of thinking to our relationships.

A cure for our human condition doesn't exist. But we can heal certain parts of ourselves. We can re-parent. We can identify our attachment styles. We can (and should) set boundaries. We can develop productive and healthy communication styles. However, pain will endure, and life's challenges will always be present. Healing in this context is not about finding perpetual happiness or the elimination of pain. Life is a journey filled with ups and downs, unexpected twists, and unforeseen challenges. There will be periods of peace, but suddenly, something devastating may occur that feels like the ground has been ripped from beneath you. Whether it's the end of a relationship, the loss of a loved one, financial setbacks, or a physical injury, life's unpredictability is a constant.

So, where do we begin?

Congratulations, babe, you've already taken the first step! And I genuinely mean it. If you are open to learning, to seeking knowledge outside yourself, that curiosity is the most valuable thing you can bring into your consciousness. A curious mindset asks the question "What can I learn about myself?" and that's a key to personal growth. Healing is a *practice*. I'm doing it now, as I write this to you. And I will do it for the rest of my life. Because I don't know everything, and neither do you. Socrates is reported to have once said, "I am wise not because I know, but because I know I don't know." Similarly, Salvador Minuchin put it best when he wrote, "Certainty is the enemy of change." And, to emphasize this point further, James Hollis says, "Doubt is the necessary fuel for change, and therefore growth." In essence, it's crucial for us to reflect and challenge ourselves. If we are unwilling to accept that our perspectives are limited and incomplete, we cannot grow or expand our understanding of the world around us. This is a radical lesson for you, me, and everyone else in the world right now. Love, sex, and relationships are subjective and context-dependent—anything but certain or universal.

But let me tell you, this actually *is* radical.

I'm not just encouraging healthy communication or conscious relationships. This isn't about taking deep breaths. (Having said that, I do hope you're still breathing.) We're not just trying to decrease or tolerate irresolvable conflict. This is the beginning of a commitment to ourselves to live in a different way. That is a big change, moving-to-another-country big change. Actually, much bigger. More like organ-transplant big.

This is a cultural movement. It's not just relationship advice. It's a complete paradigm shift. This complexity is what I want to leave you with. When my head hurts, I'll acknowledge the headache, maybe have some water or eat a carb. And if the headache doesn't go away, I'll take a Tylenol. Maybe if someone asks why I'm frowning, I'll say, "Ugh, I have a splitting headache." But I won't dwell on it all day. I won't feel shame for having a headache. I won't think that I made a mistake for having a headache. I won't start comparing my headache to the headache of some random person on Instagram. The headache will simply be a mostly neutral part of my experience.

So, too, with sadness, and relationship challenges, and sexual challenges, and tears after a breakup. We recognize sadness when we feel it. It is a multilayered experience, influenced by our perspectives on what it means, why it's there, what it says about who we are, how to deal with it, and even if we should deal with it at all. Yet, we've learned to approach these emotional challenges very differently than we do physical pain. As psychiatrist R. D. Laing has said, "There is a great deal of pain in life and perhaps the only pain that can be avoided is the pain that comes from trying to avoid pain." And this is the biggest problem we face. We live in a culture that often implies we shouldn't have problems. However, the reality is quite different—we should have many problems! And most of these so-called problems are normal when considering the context of our lives.

This is what you need to work on accepting. Within

yourself. Within your relationships. Within your body. And in the world.

We have to think about our identities. We have to think about the laws in our country. We have to think about our parents' marriage or divorce. We have to think about our childhood trauma, and our partner's or date's childhood trauma. And our parents' childhood traumas. We have to understand who was abandoned, who was enslaved, who was lost to genocide, who immigrated, and who was addicted. We have to understand our financial situation, the city we live in. We have to understand a variety of contextual clues, characters, and settings of our collective stories.

Are you constipated?

Did you sleep?

Did you eat?

It's *all* interrelated and all just as important. Mind, body, history, and culture (our environment).

The solution?

Let it all go: "Healthy" is over. Problems aren't problems. "Good versus bad" is not a thing. Instead, replace such binaries with:

A meaningful story
Opportunities to learn
Neutrality and nuance
Self-acceptance
Observation
Curiosity
Understanding
Acceptance

Tolerance

Humor

And then add some more humor

Use these nuanced approaches on yourself, on dates, with friends, and to your partners. *In all* your relationships.

You might think I'm crazy. You might be saying to yourself, *I've just read an entire book on how to be healthy in love, only to have the author tell me to forget the idea of being healthy.* Well, yes.

To clarify one last time: I am not endorsing unhealthy behaviors or condoning abuse. I'm not suggesting you do an eight ball of coke and scream at your partner. I am suggesting that when a challenge arises you welcome it. Feel everything. Resist resisting pain. Pain is part of the human experience. There is no way to avoid it. You don't have to be thrilled about it; throw a temper tantrum if you must. But you will be better served if you learn to approach your pain with kindness. Let yourself react; be as emotional as you want. And then do your best to create connections if possible—with yourself, with your partner, with this imperfect world.

If you really want to be honest with yourself, this is what being honest looks like.

Many of us go through a challenging experience and default to thinking, *Why do I have to experience this again and again?* Why? Because we're living organisms and because the journey of self-discovery and healing isn't a onetime event. It's constant and ongoing. The new insights you gain today might shift or be overpowered by big emotions that trigger you. And that is not only okay but a natural part of being alive.

This is why it is important to find a place for reflection and self-soothing—be it journaling, therapy, yoga, meditation, or anything that resonates for you. We all need a place to go for solace, repair, and understanding. We cannot do it on our own. Therapy has been the most impactful part of my journey—in being both a patient and a provider. It has entirely transformed my life. It has helped me accept myself with kindness. It's helped me confront and reconcile my past, shape my present, and move toward a better future.

Regardless if it's through therapy or another means, the journey of self-discovery has no definitive endpoint. There's no grand finale, where you will finally fully comprehend your intricate self, no point where every wound is healed, every lost piece of you recovered.

James Hollis captures this sentiment perfectly in his discussion of the self: "So we may never know it (ourselves) fully any more than a swimmer could know the ocean. . . . Hence the fragile ego must content itself with 'a sense' of Self, the Self forever unknown, unknowable."

Embrace the fact that the only definite conclusion to life is its inevitable end. It's the unpredictable contours of our existence, the uncharted twists and turns, that lend our lives their captivating and poetic beauty.

Don't get me wrong. This is all very, very hard. I'm still working on this.

I started writing this book while in a tailspin, longing for Alex and missing our relationship. Yet, I had signed a multi-year contract to recount part of my story to you. For sure, I thought my break with Alex would haunt me forever, and I wanted to put those memories behind me and move on. If I could have gotten them surgically removed, I might have.

While writing this book, I've learned more about what

triggered my primitive emotional states and the contexts that drove me to a place of desperation than I thought I would. I learned about the lack of support from the world around me and reimagined the relationship I have with myself. I had been processing this in therapy, but there is something special about taking the time to write it out. To write my story.

I know you might be left wondering, *Would you get back together with Alex? If you could go back, what would you do differently?* Mid-book, I was wondering the same thing. In fact, I had intended to devote this last chapter to the "what-if," the fantasy; to revisit old conflicts, rewriting them in my head, playing them out to see what would have happened "if only I had _____," and "if only he had _____."

But what I realized is what I knew all along. This life, my relationship, my childhood—there were parts that were incredibly hard and sad. There were parts that were beautiful and memories I will cherish forever. But there is nothing I can do but *observe* it, feel it, and let it be.

I don't need to hypothesize or speculate. I can honor myself, Alex, my mother, my brothers, and even my father for having been part of my story, for having been part of me—the good, the bad, the scary, and the pleasurable. I don't need to run scenarios in the matrix to see what could have been different if this one thing or I or he or they could have _____.

What's been more productive is focusing on what *is*. Not protesting or fantasizing about what could have been but acknowledging how things are.

And sometimes things are painful. That's just how it goes.

Figure out why you are the way you are. What happened to you? What didn't happen to you? And find a way to befriend all those parts. Honor them. Forgive other people. Forgive your-self. Never forget, but stop dwelling. Move forward. Write your story. Don't hold back. Experiment with everything. Fuck up and get it wrong. *Learn from it.* And go do it differently with your new insights.

Then yes, fuck up again. And keep up that work.

The moral of the story? Fuck the fairy tale!

This is what I want to leave you with. I want you to experience love in a different way, not just in the typical romantic or passion-ate sense. Instead, I want you to develop a love of life. And by *love,* I mean a deep appreciation for all life's ups and downs. For not just the joy of it, but also the heartbreak and sorrow. And for the powerful connections to people, places, and things.

I never loved or felt so deeply about life before Alex came into mine. Growing up, I had always hated life; I resented it. Everyone hurt me, and life felt unsafe for many years. But with Alex, I learned what it meant to be alive. And when we broke up, I felt a profound loss. I not only lost the love of a partner and a family, but also the very sense of aliveness I had discov-ered with him. I felt like I had nothing.

But then, in the process of rebuilding, I learned to appreci-ate life again. I learned to love myself. I got a dog and learned what it meant to love beyond myself. Through my work, I developed a new relationship with others as a therapist. I began to see my mother not just as a figure from my past but as a human with her own complexities—both flaws and strengths. I questioned my comfort zone and learned more than I ever thought I could.

In sessions with clients, I've been privileged to watch many discover a newfound love of and appreciation for their lives. And this is what I hope to instill in you. I want you to embark on your own journey without judgment or expectations. Find something within yourself you can understand and express that makes you feel alive and connected to our collective humanity.

Dear Reader,

I have something I need to share with you. There is absolutely, positively nothing wrong with you.

Undoubtedly, at some point, you've been hurt. Perhaps you bear deep wounds, leaving lasting scars and tender spots that stir up powerful emotions.

Often, the world fails to tell us that we're doing okay, that we're loved, important, valued. So, I want to remind you: You are all those things.

Life is tough. It is filled with beauty and wonder, but also undeniably challenging. It can be harsh, regardless of our individual context or identity. Not many acknowledge this truth, but I want to do so.

You've been a survivor since the day you were born, and you'll continue to be.

Relationships can be painful, yet they also provide the key to crafting a fulfilling life. Even if relationships occasionally breed suffering, they also foster growth. You will experience pain, love, and learning in repeating cycles. Yes, you will make mistakes, have moments of failure, celebrate victories, and stumble once again. But remember: There is nothing wrong with this or with you.

This book reflects what I learned from my own therapist, as a therapist, and as a human being navigating the same world as you. While I don't hold all the answers, I've shared what I believe could be the most beneficial insights.

I wrote this book for you. To reassure you that you're not alone, that I comprehend and share your feelings. My hope is that these words bring comfort, letting you find solace in the knowledge that your struggles are shared. I hope to inspire and empower you, to encourage you to chase your dreams without fear or loneliness as a deterrent.

I've faced my own struggles with anxiety and depression, and I still do. I know the feeling of being overwhelmed by pain. Some days, I feel a crushing loneliness; on others, I feel unexpected peace. Maybe you can relate to this; maybe not. But if you do, I hope my words make you feel slightly less alone.

Remember, I'm here with you. I'm thinking about you, wishing I could give you a reassuring hug and whisper in your ear that you're loved. I hope my words inspire you to overcome your fears and pursue your desires.

TSB

*   *   *

Now, I want you to write yourself a letter. You can make it similar to the one I wrote, but personalize it. Contextualize your life. Tell yourself the things that, at times, you can resist or shy away from. Write it all out.

Your story needs to be told. It's time to write it.

Acknowledgments

I am profoundly grateful for the chance to write this book—a long-held dream that always seemed too ambitious until one day, I decided to embrace it. Here I am, astounded and overflowing with joy and gratitude, having transformed my thoughts into words. This journey has been a healing, restorative experience, and for that, I am eternally thankful. It's hard to believe I'm here, finally expressing my thanks to all who've been instrumental in this journey.

To all my dear clients, your trust and openness have not only helped you on your healing paths but have been equally transformative for me. Our shared sessions have been a blessing, filled with authentic love and mutual growth. Your journeys are a constant source of inspiration and strength.

Derek, my therapist, mentor, and at times surrogate parent, you've been a guiding force in my life since I was fifteen. Your unwavering support and help throughout the years have been nothing short of lifesaving. I am deeply indebted to you for the love and support you've shown me throughout the years. I owe you more than words can express, for the impact you've had on both my personal and professional life is immeasurable.

To my mom, the first to show me love, laughter, and resilience amid life's chaos. Our journey together, filled with its highs and lows, has been one of profound learning and love. Dad, though our relationship was complex, and you are no longer here, your influence is an indelible part of my story.

To my dear friends, especially Lisa, Ben, Wednesday, Nicki, Montana, Tara, Dan, Sean, Dustin, and Clair—your unwavering support and love have been my anchor.

Alex, my first love, and your family, our time together taught me the meaning of love and family. You helped me grow up. The memories we've shared, both joyful and painful, will be cherished forever.

Donna, my incredible editor, your brilliance and guidance have turned this book from a dream into a reality. Your talent and support have been indispensable, and I hope our paths continue to cross. To the team at Rodale Books and Penguin Random House, your expertise and patience have made this process enjoyable and fulfilling. Taylor, your assistance and insights have been vital in shaping this book from start to finish. Bethany, your support with the proposal gave me the confidence to trust and believe in my story. You were the catalyst for this entire journey.

Andy, Andre, and Jordan, my agents and lawyer: Andy, your continued support has been a pillar of strength, thank you for turning this dream into a reality; Andre, your guidance has helped me grow in ways I never imagined; Jordan, your friendship and legal expertise have brought both ease and enjoyment to this process. Together, you've formed an incredible team.

To my online community, your words and presence have been a source of comfort and connection. Thank you for journeying with me and allowing me to be a part of your lives.

Writing this acknowledgment is but a small gesture toward the immense impact each one of you has had on my life. This book is not just my story; it's a testament to the collective journey of connection, healing, and understanding that we've shared. It is a spiritual experience, a culmination of all of life's pains and pleasures. To everyone who has ever touched my life, I owe a debt of gratitude. You have been my greatest teachers. This book is as much yours as it is mine. Thank you.

Notes

Introduction

ix **"Your vision will become"** Carl Jung, *C. G. Jung Letters,* Volume 1, ed. Gerhard Adler (London: Routledge, 1973) 33–34.

Chapter 1

3 **"Until we uncover the actual triggering event"** Mark Wolynn, *It Didn't Start with You: How Inherited Family Trauma Shapes Who We Are and How to End the Cycle* (New York: Penguin, 2017), 77.

Chapter 2

14 **"In love, happiness is an abnormal state"** Marcel Proust, *In Search of Lost Time,* Volume II, *Within a Budding Grove* (New York: Outlook Verlag, 2023), 109.

22 **Many people enact an unconscious loyalty** Term from Bert Hellinger, *No Waves Without the Ocean: Experiences and Thoughts* (Germany: Karnac Books, 2006), 197.

Chapter 3

33 **"The past is never dead. It's not even past"**   William
Faulkner, *Requiem for a Nun* (New York: Random House, 1951), 73.
35 **"I am as I am treated"**   James Hollis, *The Eden Project: In
Search of the Magical Other: Studies in Jungian Psychology by Jungian
Analysis* (Toronto: Inner City Books, 1998), 19.
42 **"good enough parent"**   D. W. Winnicott, *Playing and Reality*
(London: Routledge, 1991), 10.

Chapter 4

47 **"Sex begins in the mind"**   Michael Bader, *Arousal: The
Secret Logic of Sexual Fantasies* (New York: St. Martin's Press, 2002).
53 **Sex is not just a biological act**   This sentiment reflects
ideas expressed by various sociologists, anthropologists, and
gender theorists over the years, but without a specific source.
See Chris Donaghue, *Sex Outside the Lines* (Dallas: BenBella
Books, 2015).
53 **"The more marginalized identities"**   Alexandra Solomon, *Taking Sexy Back: How to Own Your Sexuality and Create the
Relationships You Want* (Oakland, CA: New Harbinger Publications, 2020), 105.
54 **"People who love and explore sex"**   Betty Dodson, *Sex
for One: The Joy of Selfloving* (New York: Three Rivers Press,
1996), 56.
60 **Dual Control Model of Sexual Response**   E. Janssen and J. Bancroft, "The Dual Control Model: The Role of
Sexual Inhibition and Excitation in Sexual Arousal and Behavior," in E. Janssen, ed., *The Psychophysiology of Sex* (Bloomington:
Indiana University Press, 2007), 197–222.
60 **"The problem isn't the desire itself"**   Emily Nagoski,
*Come as You Are: The Surprising New Science that Will Transform Your
Sex Life* (New York: Simon and Schuster, 2021), 245.
63 **"Tell me how you were loved"**   The quote is attributed
to Esther Perel, who has made this statement in her talks, in-
terviews, and writings on relationships, intimacy, and sexuality.
Perel is the author of several books, including *Mating in Captivity: Unlocking Erotic Intelligence* and *The State of Affairs: Rethinking
Infidelity.*

69 **"Sexual excitement requires that we"** Michael J. Bader, *Arousal: The Secret Logic of Sexual Fantasies* (New York: Thomas Dunne Books, 2002), 33.

Chapter 5

71 **"Love isn't something natural"** Erich Fromm, *The Art of Loving* (New York: Harper & Row, 1956), 56.

73 **During any external shift** The concept that external shifts can lead to changes in relationship dynamics is a common theme in relationship and couples therapy literature.

Chapter 6

90 **"It hurts to love"** Susan Sontag, *Reborn: Journals and Notebooks, 1947–1963*, ed. David Rieff (New York: Farrar, Straus and Giroux, 2008), 262.

91 **"flooded"** John Gottman, *The Science of Trust: Emotional Attunement for Couples* (New York: W. W. Norton & Company, 2011), 199.

91 **the "veracity trap"** Peter Levine, *Trauma and Memory: Brain and Body in a Search for the Living Past* (Berkeley, CA: North Atlantic Books, 2015), 25.

93 **"Someone without the marks of trauma"** Gabor Maté and Daniel Maté, *The Myth of Normal: Trauma, Illness, and Healing in a Toxic Culture* (New York: Avery/Penguin Random House, 2022), 20.

94 **"Parents have the authority to define reality"** Bader, *Arousal*, 37.

94 **"passive abuse"** Terry Real's discussion is in *Us: Getting Past You and Me to Build a More Loving Relationship* (New York: Rodale/Penguin Random House, 2022), 28.

94 **Emotional detachment, distance, and lack of connection** See Real, *Us*, 28.

94 **"You don't remember trauma"** Real, *Us*, 7.

94 **"dictate much of our behavior"** Maté and Maté, *The Myth of Normal*, 16.

94 **"We have learned that trauma is not just an event"** Bessel van der Kolk, *The Body Keeps the Score: Brain, Mind, and Body in the Healing of Trauma* (New York: Viking, 2014), 21.

95 **"can alter a person's biological, psychological, and social equilibrium"** Levine, *Trauma and Memory.*

98 *repetition compulsion* Sigmund Freud, *Beyond the Pleasure Principle*, trans. C. J. M. Hubback (London: The International Psycho-Analytical Press, 1922), 30.

103 **"The unconscious insists"** Annie G. Rogers, *The Unsayable: The Hidden Language of Trauma* (New York: Random House, 2006), 298.

107 **"No one is right"** John and Nan Silver, *Seven Principles for Making Marriage Work* (New York: Harmony Books, 1999), 157.

107 **"There is no place for objective reality"** Real, *Us*, 44.

108 **corrective emotional experience** Franz Alexander and Thomas Morton French, *Psychoanalytic Therapy: Principles and Application* (New York: Ronald Press, 1946), 66.

Chapter 7

114 **"Human beings seem to have"** R. D. Laing, *The Politics of Experience* (New York: Pantheon Books, 1967), 73.

116 **"As long as you keep secrets"** van der Kolk, *The Body Keeps the Score*, 235.

117 **"render our relationship to ourselves more conscious"** Hollis, *The Eden Project*, 13.

117 **"The distance from your pain"** Stephen Levine and Ondrea Levine, *Embracing the Beloved: Relationship as a Path of Awakening* (New York: Anchor Books, 1995), 4.

123 **introduced the concept of differentiation** Murray Bowen and M. E. Kerr, *Family Evaluation: An Approach Based on Bowen Theory* (New York: W. W. Norton, 1988); David Schnarch, *Passionate Marriage: Keeping Love and Intimacy Alive in Committed Relationships* (New York: W. W. Norton, 2012).

124 **"getting closer and more distinct"** Schnarch, *Passionate Marriage*, 56.

124 **"I want the loved person"** Fromm, *The Art of Loving*, 28.

124 **"When two become one"** Perel, *Mating in Captivity*, 25.

133 **"keeping true intimacy away"** Schnarch, *Passionate Marriage*, 39.

134 **"loveable idiot"** "Alain de Botton: On Love," lecture given at the Sydney Opera House, Sydney, 2020, YouTube video,

n.d., https://www.youtube.com/watch?v=Ctz6eJ3Pr94&ab
_channel=SydneyOperaHouse.

137 **"childhood is a gentle open prison"**   Alain de Botton,
introduction to *The School of Life: An Emotional Education* (London: The School of Life, 2019), 35.

138 **"willingness to suffer"**   Thomas S. Szasz, *The Second Sin* (Garden City, NY: Anchor Press, 1973), 15.

138 **"We can't have change without loss"**   Lori Gottlieb,
Maybe You Should Talk to Someone: A Therapist, Her Therapist, and Our Lives Revealed (New York: Houghton Mifflin Harcourt, 2019), 6.

139 **"make the unconscious conscious"**   C. G. Jung, *Collected Works of C. G. Jung*, Volume 16: *Practice of Psychotherapy*, ed. G. Adler and R. F. C. Hull, Bollingen Series XX (Princeton, NJ: Princeton University Press, 1966).

139 **"biggest tragedy of our lives"**   Tara Brach, *Radical Acceptance: Embracing Your Life with the Heart of a Buddha* (New York: Bantam Books, 2003), 23.

Chapter 8

141 **"Lovers pass constantly"**   Octavio Paz, *The Double Flame: Love and Eroticism,* translated by Helen Lane (New York: Harcourt Brace & Company, 1995).

143 **"the new shame is staying"**   Esther Perel, *The State of Affairs: Rethinking Infidelity* (New York: HarperCollins, 2017), 15.

155 **"intense erotic charge"**   Perel, *The State of Affairs,* 100.

Chapter 9

160 **"All relationships begin, and end, in separation"**   Hollis, *The Eden Project,* 11.

171 **"What is unconscious remains repressed"**   James Hollis, *Swamplands of the Soul: New Life in Dismal Places* (Toronto: Inner City Books, 1996), 87–88.

172 **"Life begins on the other end of despair"**   Jean-Paul Sartre, *Being and Nothingness: An Essay on Phenomenological Ontology,* trans. Hazel E. Barnes (New York: Philosophical Library, 1956).

172 **"How many of you are in a relationship or married?"**   "Esther Perel with Chris Cuomo: The State of

Affairs—Rethinking Infidelity," Interview conducted at the 92nd Street Y, New York, 2017, YouTube video, n.d., https://www.youtube.com/watch?v=r0dVjeBNANA.

Chapter 10

194   **"I accept myself just as I am"**   Carl Rogers, *On Becoming a Person: A Therapist's View of Psychotherapy* (New York: Harper-Collins, 2012),17.

194   **"My suffering might even be my credential"**   Sharon Salzberg, *Real Love* (New York: Flatiron Books, 2017), 32.

195   **"It is only by providing the genuine reality"**   Rogers, *On Becoming a Person*, 33.

197   **"The purpose of the very act of recall"**   Levine, *Trauma and Memory*, 141.

Chapter 11

205   **"Real love allows for failure and suffering"**   Salzberg, *Real Love*, 16.

206   **"Psychological work, instead of providing"**   Aldo Carotenuto, *Eros and Pathos: Shades of Love and Suffering* (Toronto: Inner City Books, 1989), 79.

207   **"Life is not a problem to be solved"**   Søren Kierkegaard, *The Sickness unto Death: A Christian Psychological Exposition for Edification and Awakening by Anti-Climacus*, trans. Alastair Hannay (London: Penguin Books, 2004).

208   **"Run toward pain"**   Pema Chödrön, *When Things Fall Apart* (Boston: Shambhala Publications, 2000), 68.

210   **"Certainty is the enemy of change"**   Salvador Minuchin, Michael D. Reiter, and Charmaine Borda, *The Craft of Family Therapy: Challenging Certainties* (London: Routledge, 2013), 4.

210   **"Doubt is the necessary fuel"**   Hollis, *Swamplands of the Soul*, 56.

211   **"great deal of pain"**   R. D. Laing, *The Divided Self: An Existential Study in Sanity and Madness* (London: Penguin Books, 1960).

214   **"the Self forever unknown"**   Hollis, *The Eden Project*, 16.

Index

About the Author

Todd Baratz is a renowned psychotherapist and sex therapist whose innovative approach to mental health and relationships has established him as a leading figure in his field. In addition to his clinical practice, Baratz is a prolific writer and speaker. His insights are regularly featured in various media outlets, where he discusses topics ranging from romantic relationships to individual mental wellness. He lives in New York City and Los Angeles. Learn more at toddsbaratz.com or by following him @YourDiagnonsense on Instagram.

About the Type

This book was set in Baskerville, a typeface designed by John Baskerville (1706–75), an amateur printer and typefounder, and cut for him by John Handy in 1750. The type became popular again when the Lanston Monotype Corporation of London revived the classic roman face in 1923. The Mergenthaler Linotype Company in England and the United States cut a version of Baskerville in 1931, making it one of the most widely used typefaces today.

.